Saeed Ullah Jan

An Improved Lightweight Privacy Preserving Authentication Scheme for SIP-Based-VoIP Using Smart Card

Anchor Academic Publishing

Ullah Jan, Saeed: An Improved Lightweight Privacy Preserving Authentication Scheme for SIP-Based-VoIP Using Smart Card, Hamburg, Anchor Academic Publishing 2017

Buch-ISBN: 978-3-96067-128-2
PDF-eBook-ISBN: 978-3-96067-628-7
Druck/Herstellung: Anchor Academic Publishing, Hamburg, 2017

Bibliografische Information der Deutschen Nationalbibliothek:
Die Deutsche Nationalbibliothek verzeichnet diese Publikation in der Deutschen Nationalbibliografie; detaillierte bibliografische Daten sind im Internet über http://dnb.d-nb.de abrufbar.

Bibliographical Information of the German National Library:
The German National Library lists this publication in the German National Bibliography. Detailed bibliographic data can be found at: http://dnb.d-nb.de

All rights reserved. This publication may not be reproduced, stored in a retrieval system or transmitted, in any form or by any means, electronic, mechanical, photocopying, recording or otherwise, without the prior permission of the publishers.

Das Werk einschließlich aller seiner Teile ist urheberrechtlich geschützt. Jede Verwertung außerhalb der Grenzen des Urheberrechtsgesetzes ist ohne Zustimmung des Verlages unzulässig und strafbar. Dies gilt insbesondere für Vervielfältigungen, Übersetzungen, Mikroverfilmungen und die Einspeicherung und Bearbeitung in elektronischen Systemen.

Die Wiedergabe von Gebrauchsnamen, Handelsnamen, Warenbezeichnungen usw. in diesem Werk berechtigt auch ohne besondere Kennzeichnung nicht zu der Annahme, dass solche Namen im Sinne der Warenzeichen- und Markenschutz-Gesetzgebung als frei zu betrachten wären und daher von jedermann benutzt werden dürften.

Die Informationen in diesem Werk wurden mit Sorgfalt erarbeitet. Dennoch können Fehler nicht vollständig ausgeschlossen werden und die Diplomica Verlag GmbH, die Autoren oder Übersetzer übernehmen keine juristische Verantwortung oder irgendeine Haftung für evtl. verbliebene fehlerhafte Angaben und deren Folgen.

Alle Rechte vorbehalten

© Anchor Academic Publishing, Imprint der Diplomica Verlag GmbH
Hermannstal 119k, 22119 Hamburg
http://www.diplomica-verlag.de, Hamburg 2017
Printed in Germany

WITH THE NAME OF ALMIGHTY "ALLAH" THE MOST MERCIFUL AND THE GRACIOUS

ALL GLORY BE TO ALLAH,

THE CREATOR OF THE UNIVERSE,

THE MOST MERCIFUL AND MIGHTY,

THE LORD OF THE DAY OF JUDGMENT,

THE ONLY WE WORSHIP,

THE ONLY WE ASK FOR HELP,

GUIDE US (O LORD) TO THE PATH THAT IS STRAIGHT,

THE PATH OF THOSE YOU HAVE BLESSED, NOT OF THOSE WHO HAVE EARNED YOUR ANGER, NOR THOSE WHO HAVE GONE ASTRAY

"AMEEN"

Dedication

This thesis is dedicated:

To

The Holiest Man Ever Born,

Prophet Muhammad (صلى الله عيہ وسلم)

&

To

MY Parents and Family

I am most appreciative of my parents, family and love of my life, whose affection has always been the source of encouragement for me, and whose prayers have always been a key to my success.

&

To

My Beloved colleagues

Who were always there for me and made my life at UOM easier and fun.

&

To

My Honorable Teachers

Whose are beacon of knowledge and a constant source of inspiration for my whole life span.

Acknowledgements

First of all I would like to thank ALMIGHTY ALLAH for his countless blessing to complete my studies. At the leading edge, I would like to thank my supervisor Dr. Fawad Qayum who shared a lot of his experience and ideas with me. I appreciate his professionalism, planning, and constant involvement in my research. I cherish the time we spent in discussions and in the laboratory hammering over problems. Working under him has sharpened my research skills and increased my enthusiasm to work in cryptography.

I am grateful to Dr. Sohail Abbas for his encouragement, advice, and help whenever needed. I am thankful to the Department of Computer Science Research Lab and the Software Engineering Department for offering me a fabulous environment to work and study. I would like to take this opportunity to acknowledge Dr Sohail Abbas and lab mates who made my stay at University of Malakand exciting and unforgettable. I acknowledge the help received from him on innumerable occasions. I would especially like to thank him for helping me out with various tool flows for the discussions that we had on technical as well as non- technical topics. I thank Dr Shakeel Arshad, Dr Siffat Ullah, Dr Sami Ur Rahman and Dr Sehat Ullah for working along with me on several courses and assignments.

I am grateful to Dr Ajab Khan and Dr Siffat Ullah Khan for giving me this opportunity to further my studies. I would like to acknowledge the help received from my colleague, Mr Aziz Ur Rahman, who took care of things while I was away. I would like to thank my brothers and my family for the love and encouragement I received. Without their support this thesis would not have been possible. I would like to thank my friend Mr Aziz Ur Rahman and Mr. Muhammad Salim for his prayers and for being my role model for hard work.

SAEED ULLAH JAN

Abstract

In the past few years, secure information sharing became very popular in the area of immigration, military applications, healthcare, education, foreign affairs, etc. As secure communication utilizes both wireless and wired communication mechanizations for exchanging sensitive information, so security and privacy of the information exchange cannot be easily compromised. To moderate the security, integrity, authenticity, and privacy issues related to information exchange, numerous authentication mechanisms have been recommended by different researcher in the literature in recent times, but are vulnerable to prospective security flaws such as masquerade, insider, replay, impersonation, password guessing, server spoofing, denial-of-service attacks and in addition failed to deliver mutual authentication.

In the past few years we have also seen a balanced growth in the acceptance of VoIP (Voice over IP) facilities, because the numerous Web and VoIP applications depend on huge and extremely distributed infrastructures to process requests from millions of users in an appropriate manner. Due to their extraordinary desires, these large-scale Internet applications have frequently surrendered security for other objectives such as performance, scalability and availability. As a result, these applications have characteristically favored weaker, but well-organized security mechanisms in their foundations. Session Initiation Protocol (SIP) is an application and presentation layers signaling protocol that initiates, modifies, and terminates IP-based multimedia sessions. Implementing SIP for secure communication has been a topic of study for the past decade, and several proposals are available in the research domain. However, security aspects are not addressed in most of these proposals, because SIP is exposed to several threats and faces security issue at these layers. Probes for SIP (Session Initiation Protocol) servers have been conveyed for many years, and to gather more details about these activities we simply design a scheme for SIP servers in a network and composed data about some popular attacks. What will follow is an explanation of our interpretations and guidance on how to prevent these attacks from being successful.

Biometrics a new field of research has also been materialized in this research, entitled "a three-factor authentication scheme" in which one factor is biometrics. In biometric cryptosystems the benefits of biometric confirmation are presented to basic cryptographic key supervisory systems to enhance security. Anyhow, this research delivers a general outline of the basics, permitting to biometrics as well as cryptography. This work also gives biometric cryptosystems based on iris biometrics and using smart card as well as a password for authentication.

Table of Contents

1. Introduction 1
   1.1 Overview 1
      1.1.1 One-Factor Authentication Scheme 1
      1.1.2 Two-Factor Authentication Scheme 1
      1.1.3 Three-Factor Authentication Scheme 2
   1.2 Cryptology 2
      1.2.1 Symmetric Cryptography 3
      1.2.2 Key Generation Technique 3
      1.2.3 Symmetric Encryption and Decryption 4
      1.2.4 One-Way Digital Hash-Function 4
      1.2.5 Asymmetric Cryptography 5
   1.3 Voice over Internet Protocol (VoIP) 7
      1.3.1 Session Initiation Protocol (SIP) 8
      1.3.2 H.323 11
   1.4 Smart Card 11
      1.4.1 Background of Smart Card 11
      1.4.2 Standard Selection for Smart Card 13
      1.4.3 Application of Smart-Card 14
      1.4.4 Types of Smart Card 14
   1.5 ProVerif an Automated Software Toolkit 15
   1.6 BioHashing Technique 15
   1.7 Common Adversary Model (CAM) 17
   1.8 XOR ($\oplus$) Bitwise-Operations 18
   1.9 BAN-Logic 19
   1.10 Chapter Summary 19

2. Literature Review 21
   2.1 Overview 21
   2.2 Kim and Kue Scheme 21
      2.2.1 Registration Phase 22
      2.2.2 Login Phase 22
      2.2.3 Cryptanalysis of Kim and Kue Scheme 23
   2.3 He et al.'s Scheme 23

- 2.3.1 Registration Phase 23
- 2.3.2 Login Phase 24
- 2.3.3 Authentication Phase 24
- 2.3.4 Password Change Phase 24
- 2.3.5 Cryptanalysis of He et al.'s Scheme 25
- 2.4 Das et al.'s Scheme 25
  - 2.4.1 Registration Phase 25
  - 2.4.2 Login Phase 25
  - 2.4.3 Verification Phase 26
  - 2.4.4 Password Change Phase 26
  - 2.4.5 Cryptanalysis of Das et al.'s Scheme 26
- 2.5 An's Scheme 26
  - 2.5.1 Registration Phase 27
  - 2.5.2 Login Phase 27
  - 2.5.3 Authentication Phase 28
  - 2.5.4 Cryptanalysis of An's Scheme 29
- 2.6 Park et al.'s Scheme 29
  - 2.6.1 Registration Phase 29
  - 2.6.2 Login Phase 30
  - 2.6.3 Authentication Phase 30
  - 2.6.4 Cryptanalysis of Park et al.'s Scheme 31
- 2.7 Zhu-Xu-Feng's Scheme 31
  - 2.7.1 Initial Phase 31
  - 2.7.2 Registration Phase 31
  - 2.7.3 Login Phase 31
  - 2.7.4 Authentication Phase 32
  - 2.7.5 Cryptanalysis of Zhu-Xu-Feng's Scheme 32
- 2.8 Song's Scheme 33
  - 2.8.1 Initialization Phase 33
  - 2.8.2 Registration Phase 34
  - 2.8.3 Login Phase 34
  - 2.8.4 Authentication Phase 34
  - 2.8.5 Cryptanalysis of Song's Scheme 35

2.9 Wu et al.'s Scheme [19] 35
   2.9.1 Initialization Phase 35
   2.9.2 Registration Phase 35
   2.9.3 Login & Authentication Phases 36
   2.9.4 Password or Biometrics Change Phase 37
   2.9.5 Cryptanalysis of Wu et al.'s Scheme 37
2.10 Lee et al.'s Scheme 37
   2.10.1 Registration Phase 38
   2.10.2 Login & Authentication Phases 39
   2.10.3 Password Change Phase 40
   2.10.4 Cryptanalysis of Lee et al.'s Scheme 40
2.11 Lue et al.'s Scheme 40
   2.11.1 Registration Phase 41
   2.11.2 Login & Verification Phases 42
   2.11.3 Password Change Phase 43
   2.11.4 Cryptanalysis of Lue et al Scheme 43
2.12 Tsai et al.'s Scheme [25] 43
   2.12.1 Working of Tsai et al. scheme 43
   2.12.2 The Server Registration Phase 44
   2.12.3 The User Registration Phase 44
   2.12.4 The Login and Authentication Phase 45
   2.12.5 Cryptanalysis of Tsai et al. Scheme 45
2.13 Wu-Xu-Xiong Scheme 47
   2.13.1 Registration Phase 48
   2.13.2 Login and Authentication Phases 48
   2.13.3 Password Change Phase 50
   2.13.4 Card Revocation Phase 50
   2.13.5 Cryptanalysis of Wu-Xu-Xiang Scheme 50
2.14 Lipping Zhang et al.'s Scheme 50
   2.14.1 Initialization Phase 51
   2.14.2 Registration Phase 51
   2.14.3 Login Phase 52
   2.14.4 Authentication Phase 52

- 2.14.5 Password or Biometric Updating Phase 53
- 2.14.6 Cryptanalysis of Lipping Zhang et al.'s Scheme 54
- 2.15 Zhang et al.'s Scheme 54
  - 2.15.1 Registration Phase 55
  - 2.15.2 Login and Authentication Phases 56
  - 2.15.3 Password Change Phase 58
- 2.16 Zhang et al.'s Protocol Analysis 58
  - 2.16.1 Working Procedure of the Scheme 58
  - 2.16.2 Biometric Extraction and Password Guessing Attacks 59
  - 2.16.3 User Anonymity Violation 59
  - 2.16.4 Replay Attack and Denial-of-Service Attack 60
- 2.17 Chapter Summary 60

3. Proposed Solution 61
- 3.1 Overview 61
- 3.2 Proposed Scheme 61
  - 3.2.1 Registration Phase 64
  - 3.2.2 Login and Authentication Phases 65
  - 3.2.3 Password Change Phase 67
- 3.3 Chapter Summary 68

4. Security Analysis 69
- 4.1 Overview 69
- 4.2 Formal Security Analysis 69
  - 4.2.1 BAN Logic 70
  - 4.2.2 Rules of BAN Logic 70
  - 4.2.3 BAN Method for Protocol Analysis 72
  - 4.2.4 BAN-Logic Postulates 72
  - 4.2.5 BAN Idealized Form 75
- 4.3 Proposed Protocol Analysis 75
  - 4.3.1 BAN Goals for the Proposed Scheme 76
  - 4.3.2 BAN Idealized form for the Proposed Scheme 76
  - 4.3.3 BAN Assumptions for the Proposed Scheme 76
- 4.4 ProVerif Implementation 78
  - 4.4.1 Proposed Protocol Verification Using ProVerif 78

- 4.5 Informal Security Analysis 83
  - 4.5.1 Denning-Sacco Attack 83
  - 4.5.2 Stolen-Verifier Attack 84
  - 4.5.3 Insider Attack 84
  - 4.5.4 Password Disclosure Attack 84
  - 4.5.5 Certified-Key Guarantee 84
  - 4.5.6 Man-in-the-Middle Attack 84
  - 4.5.7 Mutual Authentication 85
  - 4.5.8 Online Password Guessing Attack 85
  - 4.5.9 Offline Password Guessing Attack 85
  - 4.5.10 Biometrics Security 85
  - 4.5.11 Resist Replay Attack 86
  - 4.5.12 Strong User Anonymity 86
  - 4.5.13 Resist Denial-of-Service Attack 86
- 4.6 Chapter Summary 87

5. Performance Analysis 88
- 5.1 Overview 88
  - 5.1.1 Attack Resistance and Functionality Analysis 88
  - 5.1.2 Storage Overhead Analysis 89
  - 5.1.3 Computation Cost Analysis 90
  - 5.1.4 Communication Cost Analysis 91
- 5.2 Chapter Summary 92

6. Conclusion and Future Work 93

Bibliography 95

List of Figures

Figure- 1: Symmetric Cryptography 3
Figure- 2: Symmetric Encryption/Decryption 4
Figure- 3: A Diagrammatic Representation of Single-Way Hash Function 4
Figure- 4: Asymmetric Cryptography 5
Figure- 5: Public Key Infrastructure 6
Figure- 6: Conventional Public Key Infrastructure 6
Figure- 7: Elliptic Curve Cryptography [25] 7
Figure- 8: VoIP Application Scenarios 8
Figure- 9: SIP's Messages Structure 8
Figure- 10: Flow Chart Representation for SIP Callee 10
Figure- 11: Participants using H.323 11
Figure- 12: A Typical Smart Card 12
Figure- 13: A Ring-Shaped Smart Card 12
Figure- 14: The Chip, Dimension and Standards Selection for Smart Card 13
Figure- 15: Smart Cards Types 14
Figure- 16: ProVerif Model 15
Figure- 17: Insecure Bio-Metric Extraction 16
Figure- 18: Biometric data with hashing 16
Figure- 19: Adversary Control over Distributed System [80] 17
Figure- 20: XOR-Logic Circuit 18
Figure- 21: XOR Technique for Error Correction 18
Figure- 22: The Registration 51
Figure- 23: Login and Authentication Phases 53
Figure- 24: Iris BioHashing Technique 62
Figure- 25: Biometric Template Storing Stages 63

List of Tables

Table- 1: Notations Used for Kim and Kue Scheme 21

Table- 2: Notations Used for the Scheme 23

Table- 3: Notations Used for the Scheme 25

Table- 4: Notations Used for An's Scheme 27

Table- 5: Notations Used for Park et al.'s Scheme 29

Table- 6: Notations Used for Zhu-Xu-Feng's Scheme 31

Table- 7: Notation Used for Song's Scheme 33

Table- 8: Notations used by Wu et al.'s Protocol 35

Table- 9: Notations Used for Lee et al.'s Scheme 38

Table- 10: Notations Used for Lue et al.'s Scheme 41

Table- 11: Notation used for Tsai et al.'s Scheme 44

Table- 12: Notations used in Wu-Xu-Xiong Scheme 47

Table- 13: Notations used Lipping Zhang et al.'s Scheme 51

Table- 14: Notation Used for Zhang et al.'s Scheme 55

Table- 15: Notation used for the Proposed Scheme..64

Table- 16: Notations used by Burrows, Abadi and Needham 70

Table- 17: Protocol steps and its descriptions...75

Table- 18: The Functionality Comparison 89

Table- 19: Storage Overhead 89

Table- 20: Computational Coast Analysis of Different Schemes...91

Chapter 1: Introduction

1.1 Overview

In this era of computing and the globalization [1], people depend more and more on computer networks (Internet) compared to traditional communication. In both commercial and private sector information sharing is an essential task. So information authentication is vital for each participant. Since data authentication depends on complex cryptographic functions and algorithms for initiating the session, it is useful to discuss the authenticity of information among the participants and strongly appropriate to have a secure and robust mutual authentication scheme which can guarantee both content and correctness of the message. Authenticity of data refers to the protection of sensitive personal information from unauthorized user or changes made by an attacker, intercept and modifying the content of the message, capture and disturb the flow of data. Therefore, many authentication schemes have been proposed by different researchers at different times for the security of data.

In network communication (Internet), a major issue is the exchange of information confirmation of indigenous and foreigner consumer in the insecure distributed environment. Categorically, authentic users are extra controlling over the attackers [2]; subsequently they retain information in the internal system that is not obtainable to the impostor. Therefore, several inaccessible consumer authentication schemes are proposed for the exchange information. These protocols claimed that they are more powerful against different attacks, but these schemes still pose weakness. The authentication schemes presented so for, to preserve the security of the exchanged information, are classified as under:

1.1.1 One-Factor Authentication Scheme

The user has a secure PIN code for authenticity. The encryption and decryption of PIN code are done by some complex cryptographic algorithms. One-factor authentication scheme was introduced by Lamport in 1981 [1] to preserve the security of information. Later on, different password based authentication schemes were presented by different researchers for various applications.

1.1.2 Two-Factor Authentication Scheme

Soon it was understood that a single-factor authentication scheme can easily be broken and therefore fails to survive fully against different attacks. The main idea for two factor authentication schemes was put forward from password-based authentication scheme.

Therefore, scholars [3] introduced two factor methods for authentication to achieve more security of information exchange. In different schemes, smart card is used as a second factor together with the password for the authentication of exchanging information.

1.1.3 Three-Factor Authentication Scheme

Though, two factor authentication schemes provide enough security yet many issues are still there. Thus, researchers [3] expressed three factors authentication schemes in which biometrics in addition to password and smart card used to ensure the communication among the users to become more secure.

However, multi-factor authentication schemes are also introduced by some researchers for authenticity. But these schemes cannot be implemented due to lack of resources, counterfeit utilization of available resources and maximum communication and computational cost. The systems of today encourage lightweight operations for security, in which random numbers and a simple hash function are used.

As already discussed, keeping in view the importance of network security for the exchange of sensitive personal information over the communication line, more efforts are necessary to protect data from unauthorized user so that the legitimate users can easily access all information in open networks. As available resources in network environment are limited, it is necessary to design such cryptographic functions and mechanisms that can exactly communicate and authenticate the legal users. Some of the cryptographic mechanisms are as under:

1.2 Cryptology

Crypto is a Latin word meaning secrete [5], it is a branch of mathematics which deals with the study of secrete writing. Cryptology is mainly divided into two sub-areas:

- **Cryptography:** It is the study of information security engineering linked with mathematics. Cryptography provides us the way to trigger the most recent security schemes for information exchange over internet. It allows us to protect the distributed environment but this is very difficult field.
- **Cryptanalysis:** The concept of investigating information security system is subject to learning about the hidden facts of the infrastructure used for information sharing. The term cryptanalysis is used to break cryptographic algorithms and get access to secretes

of cipher text, even though the key is not known. The cryptography has the following main types:

1.2.1 Symmetric Cryptography

In private key cryptography, encryption or decryption is a common technique to confirm message privacy, approval, integrity and authenticity. The encryption procedure converts a quantity or some stream of bits to cipher text subject to private secrete common key [5]. However, the decryption procedures use the same private common key and the cipher text and decipherment of plain text as shown in figure-1.

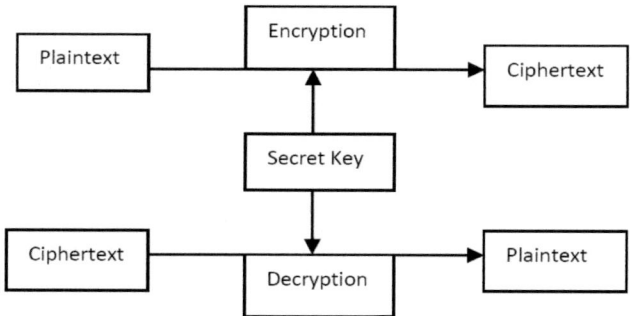

Figure- 1: Symmetric Cryptography [5]

1.2.2 Key Generation Technique

The Information Technology Laboratory (ITL) of the National Institute of Standard and Technology (NIST) has sanctioned Federal Information Processing Standard (FIPS) requiring cryptographic procedures that accepted for the Federal Government for USA use [7]. Further, NIST Specialized Proclamations (SPs) provide and suggest some proceedings that contribute the central government departments to put cryptographic algorithms in secure controlling the cryptographic important key generation which is efficiently cryptographic components which include cryptographic procedures is worn for marketable security assistance. So the key generation methodology is a step for showing proof of cryptographic algorithms.

The creation of a key is by means of several methods: RBG "Random Bit Generator" [7] is a method through which one key might be derived from another. For example, sometime a key can be generated from password and password is itself a key used for security of information. Second, private key cryptography is a common key also used for the protection of information and validation of data protection.

1.2.3 Symmetric Encryption and Decryption

Today is the age of the Internet and networks uses, achieve a great attention. The topic information security has got much significance in network communication [5]. Any harm to information might demonstrate excessive loss to organization. Encryption methods are significant in information security schemes. Formally, symmetric encryption is represented as: Let M is a message, P denotes Plain Text, E for encryption, C is cipher text and K is a private key then; E: P x K→ C and D: C x K → P. But informally we can define it, let (E, D) is a scheme that is

Cipher-Text = Encryption (Key, Message) and Message = Decryption (Key, Cipher-Text) as shown in the figure-2.

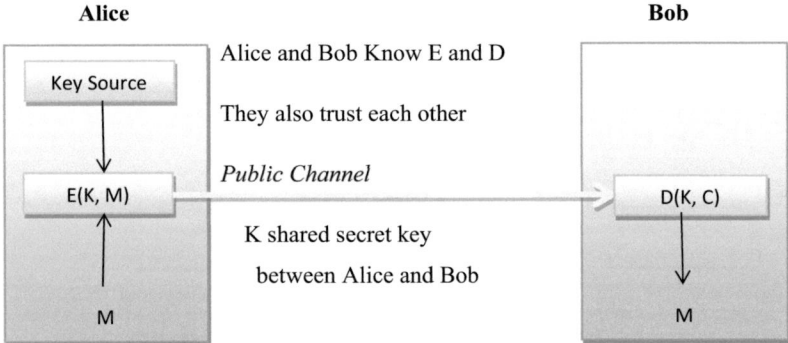

Figure- 2: Symmetric Encryption/Decryption [5]

1.2.4 One-Way Digital Hash-Function

A single-way or one-way digital hash function is a technique which converts arbitrary size text into fixed size [5]. It is represented by h (.) as shown in the figure-3 below.

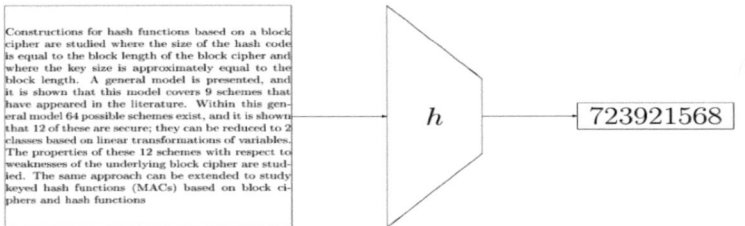

Figure- 3: A Diagrammatic Representation of Single-Way Hash Function [5]

Let suppose a message P = (P_0, P_1, P_2, ……………, P_{n-1}), the hash is h(P) = nP_0+(n-1)P_1+(n-2)P_2+……….+1.P_{n-1} and the size of the original message is a 128 bit input, then its hash be 160 bit output. This concept is called one way hash function.

1.2.5 Asymmetric Cryptography

Martin Hellman *et al.'s* [17] in 1976 designed a tremendous cryptographic technique for secrete writing and therefore named asymmetric cryptography. They attempted to develop a method for key exchange and its problem solving in symmetric cryptography. So they changed the method of single key shared between two trusted parties and develop a technique to become more related keys from the secretive one. These keys might be available publicly, but the actual one must be kept secret between the participants who create the keys. Its benefits are as under:

- Key Agreement between the parties is not needed in advance.
- The key generated party is responsible for key to be kept secret.
- Trust between the participants is direly needed in asymmetric cryptography.

Asymmetric cryptography is more secure, but heavyweight and has a maximum computational cost. Therefore symmetric cryptography technique cannot be replaced by asymmetric technique [25]. The scenarios of Asymmetric cryptography is shown in the figure-4 given below

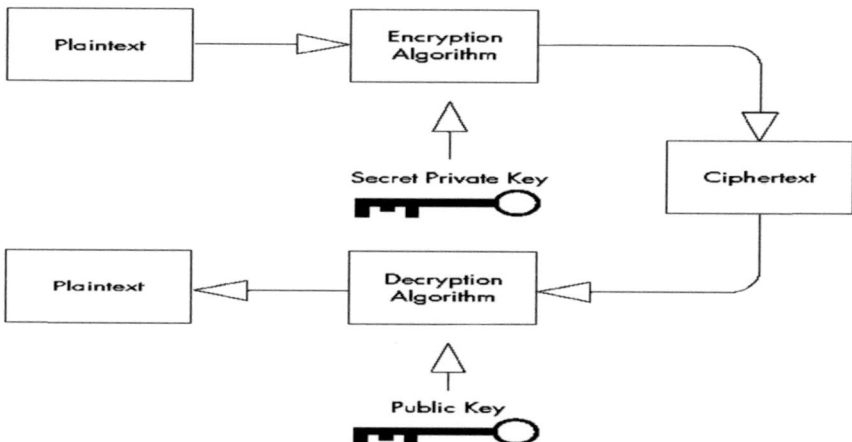

Figure- 4: Asymmetric Cryptography [25]

The public key cryptography is also referred as "Public Key Infrastructure" (PKI). It denotes the professional machineries, processes, services mutually deliver an agenda for expressing the above mentioned security mechanisms-authenticity, authorization, authentication, privacy preserving techniques and integrity of data. PKI motivate the professionals and trades to utilize the internet resources securely. For example secure, legal and mandatory mails, banking transactions, network based businesses and facilities provided might be handled by using Public Key Infrastructure as shown in the figure-5 below:

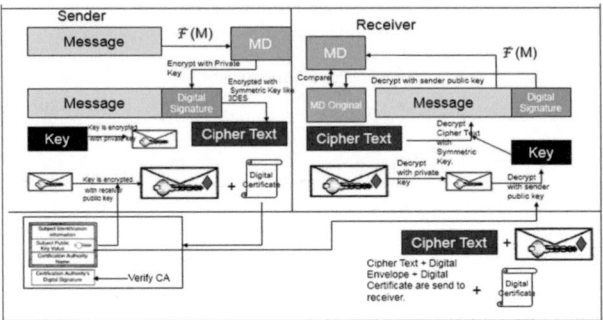

Figure- 5: Public Key Infrastructure [25]

- **CPKI:** Conventional Public Key Infrastructure a one of popular Infrastructure's available now-a-days. This infrastructure contains "Rivest-Shamir-Adleman" (RSA), "ElGamal" procedure and "Digital Signature Algorithms" (DSA) [73]. Rivest-Shamir-Adleman (RSA) is one of the biggest and most common procedures, which entrust on a big numeral factorization complication. Rivest-Shamir-Adleman (RSA) algorithm can also be used for both integrity and numerical autographs, while the ElGamal algorithm is established on isolated logarithm in a determinate numerical area and Digital Signature Algorithm used only for digital signature as shown in the figure-6 below.

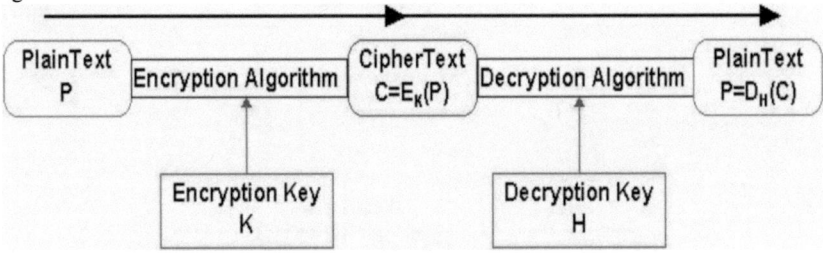

Figure- 6: Conventional Public Key Infrastructure [25]

- **ECC:** A new technique has been introduced for, security called ECC [25]. It takes more attention due to its less processing and lightweight. If not lightweight, then symmetric cryptography, one operation of ECC equal to 10 operations of symmetric Cryptography. The Rivest-Shamir-Adelman's key size [73] increases in current years, which suffer from a heavy load and maximum computational cost. The new technique is called ECC and is represented by cubic equations similar to the equation used for measuring the circumference of an ellipse.

$$q^2 + pqr + bq = p^3 + cp^2 + dp + e$$

Where p, q and r represent variables while a, b, c, d, and e are real numbers.

$$q^2 = p^3 + ap + b$$

Take another point O which is either infinity or zero, then the equation become

$$q = \sqrt{p^3 + ap + b}$$

The concept of Elliptic Curve Cryptography is shown in figure-7

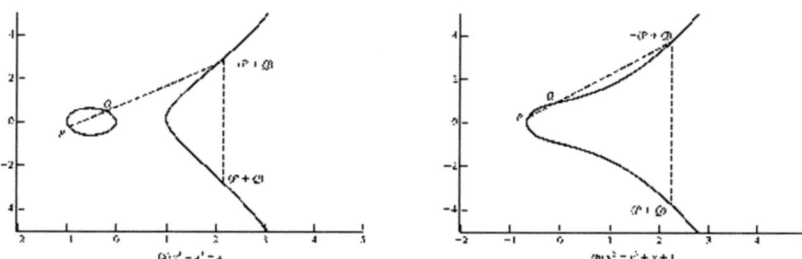

Figure- 7: Elliptic Curve Cryptography [25]

1.3 Voice over Internet Protocol (VoIP)

It is the actual period collaborative phonic, graphic, picture type submission which permits communication between two parties over the parcel-diverted network. It also allows us to make phone calls over a broadband internet connection. VoIP [74] requires that the two sides must be connected to the Internet. Another type of VoIP is designed for traditional landline/telephone. Though VoIP uses maximum for typical user yet faced potential vulnerabilities. The Scenarios of VoIP are shown in figure-8:

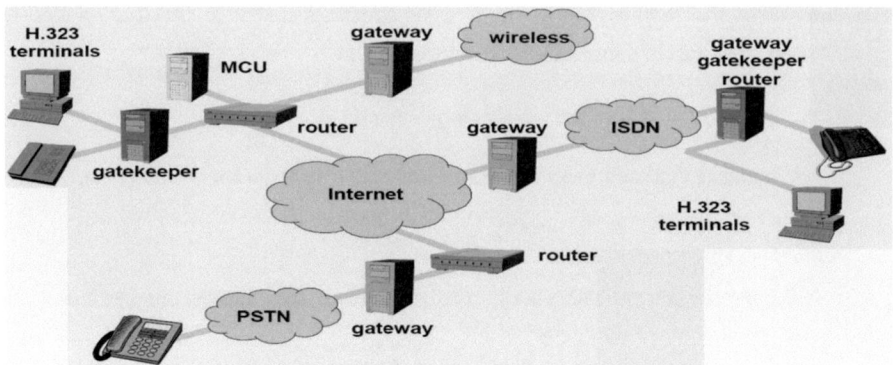

Figure- 8: VoIP Application Scenarios [74]

Two schemes have been designed for handling the fore-mentioned communication protocol: One is a Session Initiation Protocol (SIP) and the other is H.323. The detailed discussions are as under:

1.3.1 Session Initiation Protocol (SIP)

This scheme was designed by the "Institute of Electronics and Telecommunication Engineers" (IETE) in the late 90s [75]. This scheme works on the application layer that handles, controls, manages and terminates a session between computers. I should be used to fix cooperative or multimedia sessions like conversation and video conferencing. It's a text based scheme like "Hyper Text Transfer Protocol" (HTTP) use messages [75]. The structure of SIP message consists of six portions as shown in figure-9

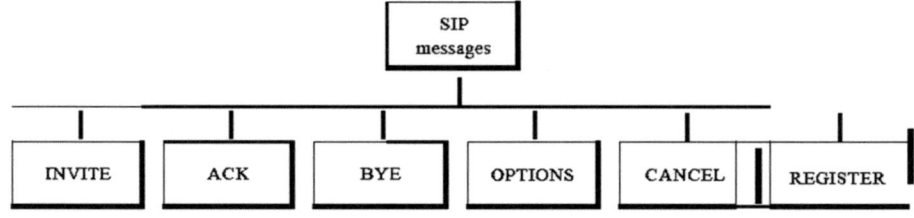

Figure- 9: SIP's Messages Structure [75]

- INVITE-Participation of any peer (user or server) for call session.
- ACK-Final response confirmation for server.
- BYE-Call termination of Callee.
- OPTIONS-Interrogation the experiences of servers.

- CANCEL-Pending work cancellation, no termination of already accepted the call
- REGISTER-Record-keeping in the header of SIP Server.

The VoIP is used to refer to audio, video and multimedia communication. This communication commence over IP networks. It is due to the fact that VoIP can easily be implemented and it is cost effective for the end user. To sustain quick evolution and usage flexibility VoIP system need efficient, flexible and secure communicating and indicating scheme. For transmitting audio, video and multimedia streams over IP networks; a real time protocol is much needed. The Session Initiation Protocol (SIP) [75] was designed for the purpose mentioned above. SIP establishes, modifies and terminates sessions among the peers. SIP provides real time between participants to set-up, modify and terminate sessions among two or more computers for the exchange of data. SIP mainly developed for five specific elements. These supported facts are: session establishment, user availability, user capabilities, location of the user and manage, control, modify, transfer of data and session termination etc. as shown in figure-9 above.

1.3.1.1 SIP Architecture

SIP is working on the application-layer [75]. Typically SIP-based signaling protocol involves the following elements:

- **User Agent:** This portion is designed for creating request and response processing.
- **Registrar:** It is a database portion of the SIP comprising localities as well as client preferences.
- **Proxy:** It receives requests and precedes it to the existing locality in the communication.
- **Redirect:** The server catches request and acknowledges the client about the incoming node.

Security of messages transmitted in SIP-based-VoIP is a challenging technique, especially whenever the session between two peers are established. The SIP-based-VoIP [76] networks need a security mechanism for the protection of information; that no one could modify, listen, and session disturbance and so forth. These kinds of vulnerabilities can exist either at signaling phase or in the communication of data (voice) phase. Therefore, both the phases use special cryptographic mechanism for protection. The architecture for understanding calling using SIP is shown using flow chart by the following figure-10

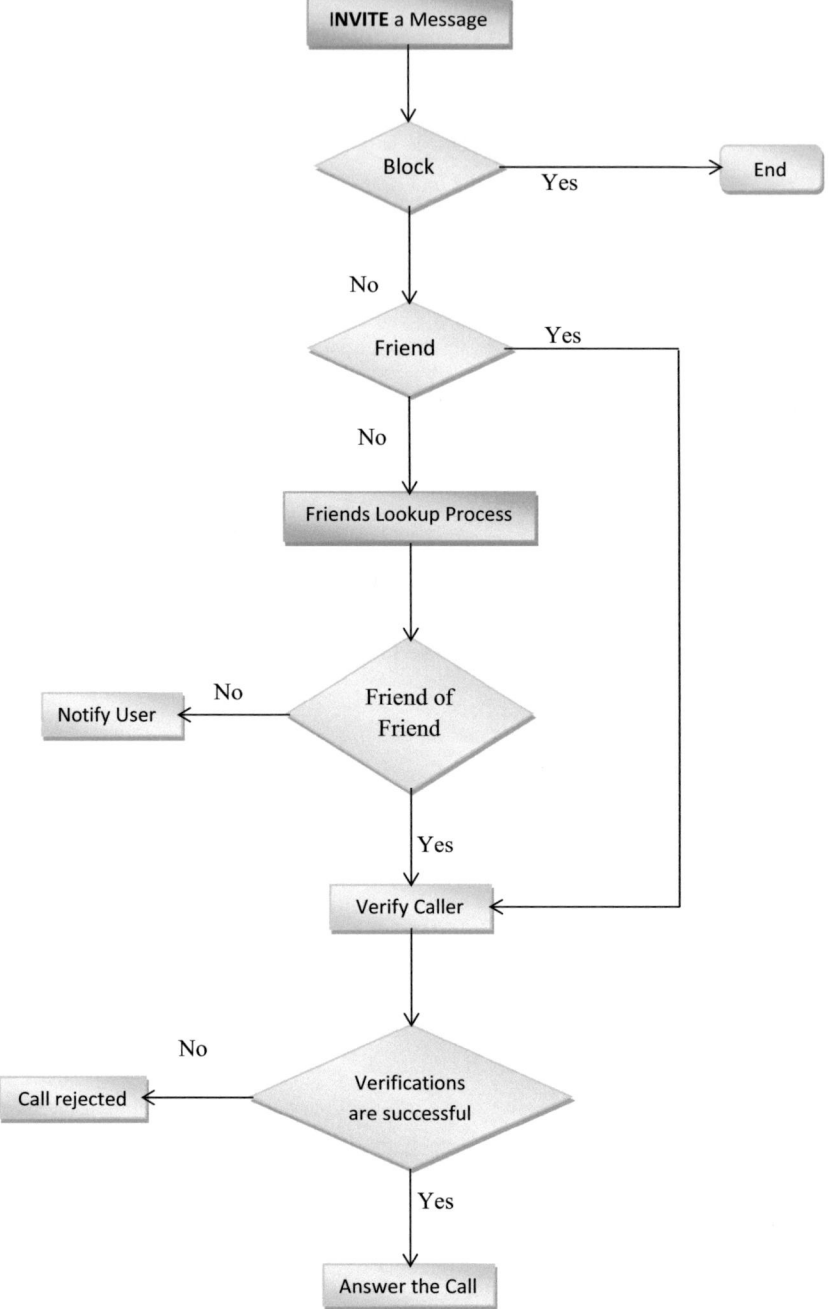

Figure- 10: Flow Chart Representation for SIP Callee

1.3.2 H.323

This is another protocol designed for VoIP. This protocol is also for the transmission of real time audio/video and multimedia communication over a VoIP network. It might be useful for other procedure like IP telephony [77], video-chatting and multipoint mixed communications. It also provides the same affection like SIP and can also be applied in a vast variety of areas- customer, trade and enjoyment purposes as shown in figure-11 below:

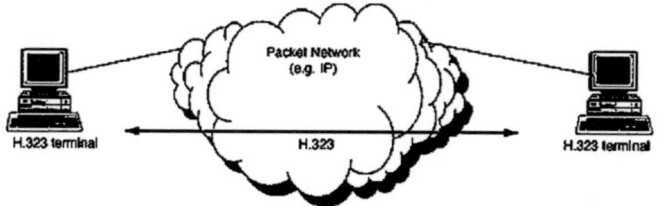

Figure- 11: Participants using H.323 [77]

It is necessary for everyone that SIP uses simple style then H.323 [77]; provides the facility of call wait-service, promoting the answer properly, easily implemented, unknown caption is ignored in SIP and using instructions of extensively used HTTP and SMPT.

1.4 Smart Card

During the last decade, smart cards have achieved an increasing appreciation as an important tool for protection, certification and agreement. The term smart card frequently deliberates to a malleable license—with the measurement of normal credit card size—having CPU that clutches microprocessor and data-storage portion talented for protection, supervision, calculating, association and accomplishment of cryptographic utilities on a remarkable capacity of storage for both assessment and confirmation [78]. These cards have indistinguishable electrical communications outlining electrical power and with outside terminals. In other words, the smart card is a microchip that encloses a CPU and some space for storage packages—e.g. ROM and EEPROM. It is an extra-small digital device having its own functional scheme, platforms and some sort of data. Contact to data in smart card for performing a task is under the supervision of the small Operating System.

1.4.1 Background of Smart Card

Several advantages of smart card have originated to reality which can expresses smart-card details, which inaugurated in the late 1960s [78].

Two German inventors, Jurgen Dethloff and Helmut Group invented the first smart-card in 1968, untested their impression by means of plastic cards along with microchips. Nevertheless, up to 1976 and the semiconductor industry, the researcher were accomplished of manufacturing chip cards for satisfactory prices. So, the primary field trials happened in 1981 to finance transactions chip card. Later, France Telecom introduced the leading phone chip in 1984. Then, the card extent concluded to other portions of Europe to bank card trial in Norway. Other Republics and business organizations also originated MasterCard's and Visa Cards for providing services to their citizens in different fields. In maximum circumstances, smart card looks like a magnetic-stripe card, but it has a microprocessor chip in the upper-left-hand corner. A typical IBM [78] made smart card is shown in figure- 12 below:

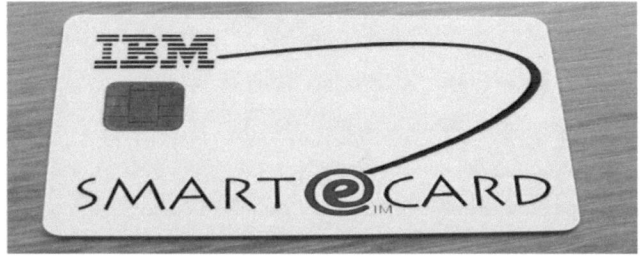

Figure- 12: A Typical Smart Card [78]

Certain smart cards originated "disguised" in a diverse form like as ring shaped (Semiconductor's Java Ring or ring-shaped smart "card" as shown in figure-13 [78]). It doesn't seem to have a chip or CPU. Completely smart cards, though, have shared structures: its own operating system for managing contact to the card's credentials, data and cryptographic tasks which are in ROM, data in EEPROM and RAM for parsing results. Normally, the CPU of smart card (old form) is 8-bit alternate—although some is 16-bit and 32-bit is also available in the marketplace.

Figure- 13: A Ring-Shaped Smart Card [78]

1.4.2 Standard Selection for Smart Card

The "International Organization for Standardization" (ISO) agrees the physical features, dimension, interaction location, electrical signals, lengthwise low-level passage and high-level presentation communication protocols [78]. Part 4 of ISO 7816 is specific attention as it identifies the typical communication-protocol statistics elements and "Application Protocol Data Units" (APDU). Furthermore, ISO 7816-4 pronounces that where the data storage part will be on a smart card and where can be planned for a file system. It also demonstrated the addressing assigning to smart cards parts such as number systems and registering techniques for smart-card requests, identifier length-value, data configurations, improves smart-card instructions, mutual authentication, SQL Query Access, encryption/decryption and many more which are shown in figure-14.

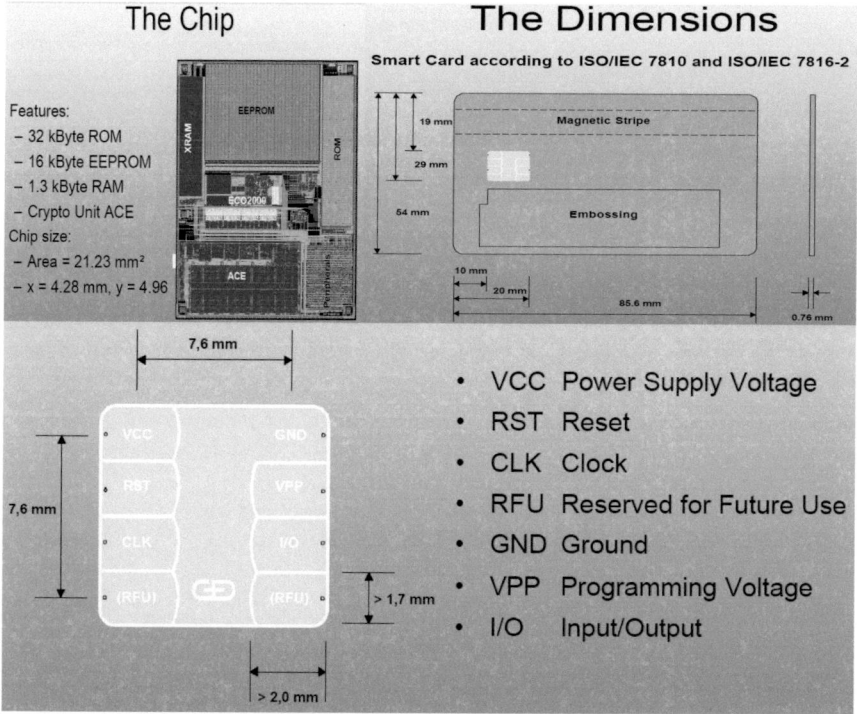

Figure- 14: The Chip, Dimension and Standards Selection for Smart Card [78]

1.4.3 Application of Smart-Card

Smart Card is responsible for performing multiple tasks, the operator incomes only one card for certain requirements. There are many applications of a single smart card; some of these are healthcare, ATM cards for banking money transaction, network usage, calling cards, Identification of a specific location, mobile phone SIM subscriber, ticketing and ringing, passports, voting system and information security etc.

1.4.4 Types of Smart Card

The smart cards can be categorized into four types:

1.4.4.1 Contact Smart Cards:

This type of smart card required physical contact with the chip e.g. money exchange cards and intelligently access sanative location for different purposes.

1.4.4.2 Contactless Smart Cards:

Contactless smart cards don't require physical contact with a device or chip however can run or empowers via radio repetition, e.g. access control, nearby open transportation system, ski passes, tickets and stuff recognizable proof.

1.4.4.3 Hybrid Smart Cards:

Hybrid smart card is a type of smart card having two chips associated with each other, one support contact interface and other contactless interface.

1.4.4.4 Dual-interface smart cards:

Double interface card is a type of smart card that contains a self-contained chip that supports both contact and contactless interfaces.

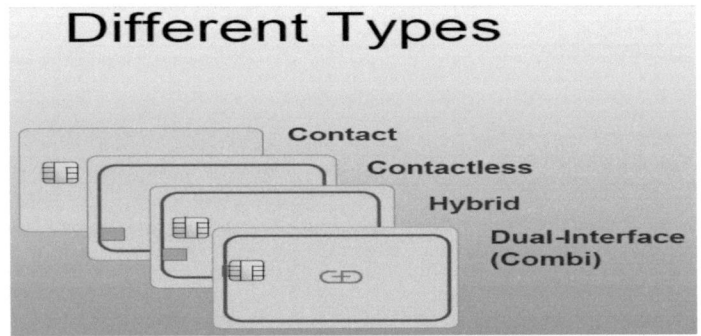

Figure- 15: Smart Cards Types [78]

1.5 ProVerif an Automated Software Toolkit

A ProVerif [18] is an automated software tool using to verify that either the designed scheme is secured against known attacks or there exists security flaws. This tool was first developed by researchers in 2001. It authenticates any new scheme for an infinite number of sessions and an infinite number of message space. It automatically and effectively investigates the authentication and security of cryptographic function related schemes used in automatic internet based exchange of information. The ProVerif also facilitate the reach-ability characteristics like confidentiality, integrity and authorization that are beneficial for security commitments of the scheme.

ProVerif tool is implemented for statistical, arithmetic and logic procedures. It uses practical pi (π) calculus for recognizing analysis of the protocol; π calculus is also used to authenticate the accuracy and strength of the designed protocol. This software tool contains three portions: declaration portion, process portion and main portion. In the first part, cryptographic basics are specified while in the second part, the procedures and sub-procedures are defined and in the last core portion fundamental steps of the scheme are defined. Our scheme is using this tool for implementation as shown in figure-16 below:

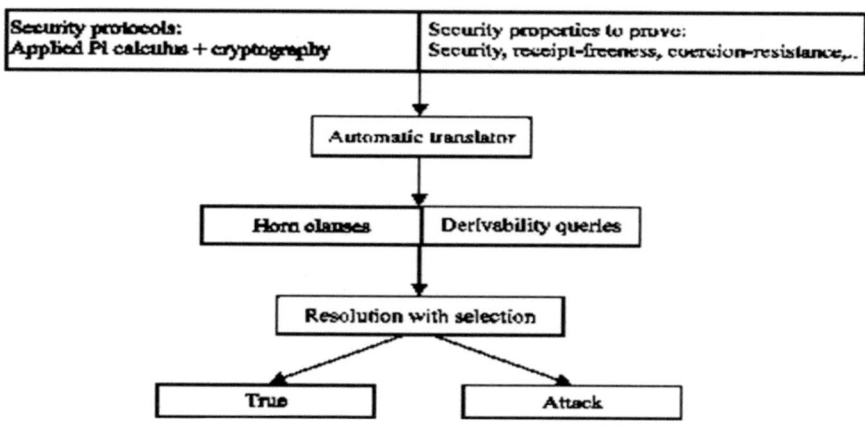

Figure- 16: ProVerif Model [18]

1.6 BioHashing Technique

Evidence of a recognizable human being, who can recognize direct or indirect, by position or by credentials quantity; to one or more factors personal to his/her physical, functional, intellectual, commercial, traditional or social individuality e.g. layout, finger-print, Iris-scan, retina-imaging, skin and facial structure. In case, someone negotiates the aforementioned characteristics of another one, a BioHashing Technique [79] is adopted. It is simple and pseudo-random sketching technique that is irreversible and can be generated using the private key. For example… figure-17 and 18 best explains the phenomenon of Bio-Hashing

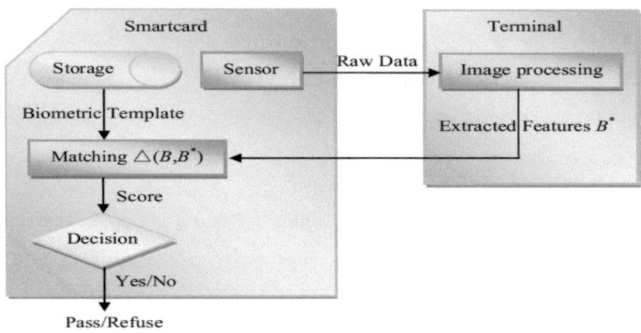

Figure- 17: Insecure Bio-Metric Extraction [79]

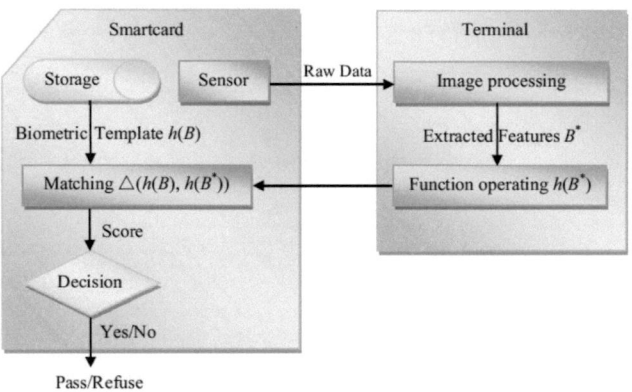

Figure- 18: Biometric Data with Hashing [79]

In other words, biometrics is a unique quantifiable characteristic to identify, designate or recognize human being. Now-a-days numerous authentication schemes are being introduced due to the explicit user codes are available like BioHashing codes. BioHashing confirmation is proper and well-matched methods that can operate anyone using smart cards or smart cell phone. In the proposed scheme biometrics is a third-factor for authentication. Before storing the biometric characteristics template in smart card, it should pass from the stage of BioHashing. So that it might provide better security compared to other authentication scheme.

1.7 Common Adversary Model (CAM)

Needham/Schroeder in 1978 put forward the concept of the Common Adversary Model that, "We assume that an intruder can interrupt a computer in all communication paths, and thus can alter or copy parts of messages, replay messages, or emit false material."

In the Common Adversary Model [80] the adversary is represented by X let suppose then....

1. X can fully control over the network, has the skill to interfere the channel, copy and replay the messages, change, eliminate or can send a fake copy of the message.
2. X can also cut evidences, broken information on smart card by showing mechanism investigation or leak out information.
3. X can either an insider or a fake expert or shows itself is a server.
4. The X and legal server are not secure and are known to all insiders.
5. The legality of the server summarized by secret key and X cannot conceal server secret key as shown in the figure-13 below.

The proposed authentication scheme provides a detailed sketch of CAM in our scheme. Formal and informal security analysis of scheme is using CAM, available in the rest of chapters.

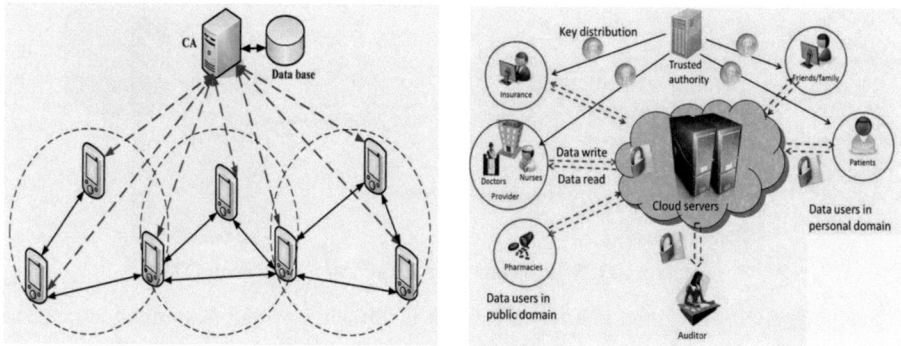

Figure- 19: Adversary Control over Distributed System [80]

1.8 XOR (⊕) Bitwise-Operations

XOR is named as exclusive-OR is used in digital circuit designing. This type of logic circuit is mostly beneficial for mathematical operations and error-detection and correction in data communication. XOR takes 2 or 3-inputs. It uses the symbol ⊕ and has the following mathematical operation/equation:

$$X \oplus Y = X Y' + X' Y$$

The logic bitwise operation of XOR (⊕) gate is given below:

$0 \oplus 0 = 0$ $\qquad$ $0 \oplus 1 = 1$ $\qquad$ $1 \oplus 0 = 1$ $\qquad$ $1 \oplus 1 = 0$

Diagrammatic representation of an XOR logic circuit is shown in figure-20 below:

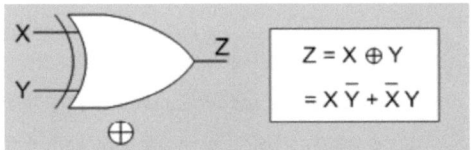

Figure- 20: XOR-Logic Circuit [25]

XOR operations are very beneficial in scheme using corresponding bits for fault discovery through the broadcasting of binary data. The message having this operation, whenever conveyed is checked at the receiving end for necessary errors. If the parity doesn't match, an error is detected as shown in the figure-21 below:

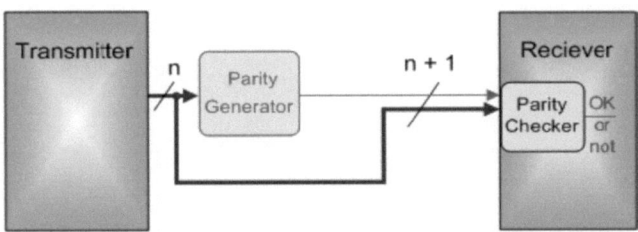

Figure- 21: XOR Technique for Error Correction [25]

Similarly, XOR-encryption is a technique that is difficult to break also called basic-power methods. In this method the encrypted text called cipher text cannot breakdown easily because it using random keys for encryption and find the exactly one for whom it designed. The XOR-Operation is used in symmetric encryption. It uses a special algebra for decryption called Boolean algebra. If a single entity in the information exchange is true then the XOR-function will return true.

1.9 BAN-Logic [16, 28]

Protocols are the means of security in many shared environment, and is therefore crucial to confirm that these schemes working efficiently or not. Unhappily, their architecture has been intensively bugs prostrate. While authentication schemes normally have short messages. The configuration of these messages might be refined and the relations among it could be difficult. Furthermore, scheme architect frequently confused the existing methods; imitate features from available schemes mistakenly. Appropriately, several of the schemes inaugurate in research hold conciseness or scrutiny pitfalls, to sum to mortification, schemes follow another type of cryptosystem and furnish for an extensive kind of utilizations; it is sometimes fair how these schemes associate in the assurance they attempt.

The aim of proof might be specified a bit easily, yet consistently and impressively. Once proof is done between two participants, two leading (participants, systems, services) must be allowed to trust each other that they make a communication and never with an interrupter. The firm using a successful authentication scheme for communication must ask these questions:

- ✓ The scheme you design for us work or not?
- ✓ Might it be complete or not?
- ✓ Can necessary changes in the scheme are possible like other schemes?
- ✓ Can the designed scheme do some needless things?

All the aforementioned difficulties, questions and risks about a robust authentication scheme can be solved using BAN Logic. The proposed scheme use BAN logic for authentication in the later chapters.

1.10 Chapter Summary

Information security has skillful and a vast developmental concept and as growing quick acceptance for the last few years. Due to their extraordinary necessities, these large-scale SIP-based-VoIP requests have frequently surrendered safety for other objectives such as presentation, scalability and accessibility. As a result, these requests have characteristically ideal weaker but extra effective security tools in their set-ups.

Chapter 1   Introduction

Due to the growing acceptance of large-scale SIP-based-VoIP applications, many authentication protocols have been demonstrated for controlling the security vulnerabilities during communication because the adversaries are now aiming and abusing the different weaknesses in these authentication mechanisms. Although many strong authentication protocols have been suggested, utmost of them fail to report the particular requests and vulnerable the large scale Internet applications and, as a result, they have not been commonly used. In this chapter the title of the thesis has been explained in detail. Practically, all concepts are implemented in the later chapters.

Chapter 2: Literature Review
2.1 Overview

Lamport [1] an information security expert in 1981 designed a scheme for exchanging information between participants, which was based on passwords. The scheme gains much popularity due to its simplicity and convenience. The scheme was later modified for various applications. The password based scheme, however have many drawbacks like password verifier maintenance table in the server and online/offline prediction of password by an attacker. To overcome these weaknesses and further modified its robustness, another two researchers Wu and Chang [2] in 1993, presented two factors remote user authorization protocol together smart card used along with a password for authentication. Due to benefits of smart cards, its portability, cryptographic functionality, low cost, processing capacity and durability, password and smart card-based authentication mechanism has become widely used, and many researchers proposed different protocols of this type for different purposes.

2.2 Kim and Kue Scheme

Kim and Kue [4] presented a scheme grounded on simple hashed function, password and symmetric encryption/decryption for the authentication of messages. They described their scheme in two steps; given below:

Symbols and its Description

- U for User, S for Server, and A means an Adversary.
- $h(.)$ a one-way secure hash
- m for message
- $h(m)$ means that the information hashed once,
- $h^2(m)$ means that the information hashed twice
- N for an integer values beginning with one (1) whenever the user is first registered.
- P for user password.
- X_S for server secret-key.
- t for timestamp or freshness.
- $\oplus$ For XOR operation,
- || for concatenation.
- U→S: V   U transmits V to S through public channel
- U⇒ S: V   S transmits V to S through private channel

Table- 1: Notations Used for Kim and Kue Scheme

2.2.1 Registration Phase

In this phase of Kim's protocol, the following steps are performed:

I: User U transmits a message over the line for registration to the remote server S.

II: S→U: d; t

The remote server S establishes "t" the present timestamp. At the first registration, the server S determined d = One, else S sets d = 1+d. Next, the server transmits "d" and timestamp "t" to the legitimate user.

III: U⇒S: $h^2(S\|P\|d\|t)$.

IV: Server calculates user's stored key $X_U^{(t)}=h(U\|h(X_S\|t))$ and verify $X_{su}^{(d)}=h^2(P\|S\|d\|t)\oplus X_U^{(t)}$; and stored $X_{su}^{(d)}$, d, and "t" in a file at the user smart card memory.

2.2.2 Login Phase

In this phase of Kim's protocol contains the following points of computation:

I: The legitimate user sends login request to the remote server.

II: S→U: r, d, t

The server chooses an arbitrary number r, saves the parameters in a file on the server.

III: U→S: Z_1, Z_2, Z_3

The user sends Z_1, Z_2 and Z_3 to S, and performs the following calculations:

$Z_1 = h^2 (Q\|S\|d\|t) \oplus h(Q\|S\|d\|t)$,

$Z_2 = h(S\|Q\|d\|t) \oplus h^2(S\|Q\|d + 1\|t)$ and

$Z_3 = h(h^2 (Q\|S\|d + 1\|t)\|r)$.

IV: The remote server calculates $X_U^{(t)}=h(U\|h(X_S\|t))$, then transmit $h^2(Q\|S\|n\|t)$ from the already available verified values $X_{su}^{(d)}$ by $h^2 (Q\|S\|d\|t) = X_{su}^{(d)} \oplus X_U^{(t)}$, and calculate u_1 and u_2 parameters i.e.

$u_1=Z_1\oplus h^2 (Q\|S\|d\|t)$

   $=h(Q\|S\|d\|t)$ and

$u_2=Z_2\oplus u_1$

   $=h_2(Q\|S\|d + 1\|t)$.

If the equation $h(u_1)=h^2(Q\|S\|d\|t)$ and $h(u_2\|r)=Z_3$ satisfy each other, then the server validates the user. Else, the server discards the user login demand and ends the process. But if holds the confirmation, the server calculates another values from these $X_{su}^{(d+1)}=u_2\oplus X_U^{(t)}=h^2(S\|Q\|d + 1\|t)\oplus X_U^{(t)}$ equations and changes $X_{su}^{(d)}$ with $X_{su}^{(d+1)}$ for renewing user whenever become boot up at another time. The value of the timestamp is unaffected.

2.2.3 Cryptanalysis of Kim and Kue Scheme

The authentication protocol of Kim and Kue above is much important for security purposes because they pretended that it could prevent all the possible security flaws; but later in 2006 some researchers found impersonation, sever spoofing, masquerade and stolen-verifier attacks.

2.3 He et al.'s Scheme

He et al.'s [5] crypt-analyzed Wu et al.'s [6] protocol and claimed that their scheme violates user anonymity. The attacker can easily lunched impersonation attack and replay attacks on the scheme. They presented a robust authentication method for wireless network having smart card. Their scheme involved four entities: foreign agent, home agent, trusted authority and cell phone user. The scheme is as under:

Symbols and its Description			
U_m	Mobile User	S_m	Main Server
R_m	Foreign Agent	ID_A	User's Identification
T_A	Timestamp	$h(.)$	Secure hash
$\|\|$	Concatenation	$\oplus$	X-OR operation

Table- 2: Notations Used for the Scheme

2.3.1 Registration Phase

The mobile user U_m chooses password PW_U, an arbitrary digit "d" and calculates $h(PW_U \oplus d)$, the below computations are performed during registration:

a. U_m at this stage calculates:
$$TX_U = h(ID_U \| X_S)$$
$$SX_U = h(ID_U \| d)$$

"X_S" and "d" define two secret numbers

b. S_m at this stage calculates:
$$r = TX_U \oplus ID_S \oplus (ID_U \| e)_n$$ Where "e: is another secrete number

$\{TX_U, SX_U, h(.), r\}$ ⟶ into the memory of smart card

c. Then U_m calculates
$$SX^*_U = h(ID_U \| h(PW_U)) \oplus SX_U,$$

$V_U = TX_U \oplus h(ID_U \| h(PW_U \oplus d))$ and

$H_U = h(TX_U)$

Finally the memory of a smart card has $\{V_U, H_U, SX^*_U, h(.), d, r\}$

2.3.2 Login Phase

The user inserts smart card in a terminal and inputs ID_U and PW_U. The terminal and card execute the below computations:

$T^*_U = V_U \oplus h(ID_U \| h(PW_U \oplus d))$,

$H^*_U = h(TX^*_U)$,

$SX_U = h(ID_U \| h(PW_U)) \oplus SX^*_U$ and produce

$E = (h(ID_U) \| ID_R \| x_0 \| x)_l$,

$d = r \oplus TX_U = ID_R \oplus (ID_U \| e)_d$,

$L = h(T_U \oplus SX_U)$ and transmits

$m_1 = \{d, E, ID_R, T_U\}$ to R_m.

2.3.3 Authentication Phase

The R_m directs a message $m_2 = \{b, n, E, T_R, T_R, E_{SR}, (h(b, n, E, T_U, T_R, Cert_R)), Cert_R\}$ to U_m. The S_m confirms whether the credentials $Cert_R$ and T_R are valid. If not, U_m dismisses the calculations; otherwise, U_m confirms the authorization of S_m by means of R_m's open key X_R. If authorization of S_m is found illegal, U_m discards the message; otherwise, U_m perform, $W = E_{PR} (h(h(d \| ID_U)) \| X_0 \| X)$, S_m sends $m_3 = \{c, W, T_{HA}, E_{SHA}, (h(b, c, W, T_S, Cert_S)), Cert_S\}$ to R_m and R_m first verify the freshness T_S is dying-out or not. If T_S is dead-out, R_m rejects the message, otherwise, R_m confirms the authorization of U_m by means of R_m's public key P_R. If the authorization of U_m found illegal, R_m discards; else, R_m decrypts "W" by using the available symmetric key S_R to get $h(h(h(d \| ID_U)) \| X_0 \| X)$. U_m, then calculates the session secrete key x and decrypts $(TCert_U \| h(X_0 \| X))_x$. If the computation of both sides is valid, U_m approves that R_m authenticated by S_m.

2.3.4 Password Change Phase

The U_m inserts his or her smart card in the terminal and provides ID_U and PW_U. Smart card and terminal then executes the following set of equations:

$TX^*_U = V_U \oplus h(ID_U \| h(PW_U \oplus m))$, $H^*_U = h(TX^*_U)$,

$SX_U = h(ID_U \| h(PW_U)) \oplus SX^*_U$ and produces

$E = (h(ID_U) \| ID_R \| X_0 \| X)_l$,

$N = r \oplus TX_U = ID_S \oplus (ID_U \| m)_l$ and

$L = h(T_U \oplus SX_U)$.

Upon confirming, U_m provides another PW_{new}. Else the smart card rejects the demand and the processes become wind-off.

2.3.5 Cryptanalysis of He et al.'s Scheme

Yang et al.'s [23] picked out that Shen et al.'s [24] scheme couldn't provide security for counterfeit attack and designed bilinear combination which established user authentication. However, the He et al.'s protocol is not user approachable i.e. the user doesn't choose and updated password easily, and also it cannot complete mutual authentication and security for a session key, which are the main possessions.

2.4 Das et al.'s Scheme

Das et al.'s [10] designed an information security protocol. The detail sketch of their scheme is explained as under:

	Symbols and its Descriptions		
U_i	User	PW_{ia}	User's Password
S	Server	h(.)	Secure on way digital hash function
$\oplus$	X-OR	N_i	A nonce value

Table- 3: Notations Used for the Scheme

2.4.1 Registration Phase

The user selects password PW_{ia} and the following steps are performed during this phase:
- The nonce N_i be obtained by calculating $h(PW_{ia})$ and $h(x)$ i.e. $h(PW_{ia}) \oplus h(x)$, x is a private key for encryption/decryption.
- Identifies those values which are stored in the smart card, i.e. h (.), D_i, PW_{ia}
- $S \Rightarrow U_i$: Password: means the remote server sends password to the user over a secure channel.

2.4.2 Login Phase

Whenever the user wants to login into the remote server; the following computations are performed during this phase:

- ✓ $CD_i = h(PW_{ia}) \oplus h(d_i \oplus y \oplus t)$
- ✓ $Z_i = h(CID_i \oplus h(PW_{ia}))$
- ✓ $Y_i = h(t \oplus d_i \oplus Z_i \oplus y)$
- ✓ $U_i \to S : CID_i, d_i, Y_i, t$

2.4.3 Verification Phase

The verification of validity of data freshness, using timestamps, ((Current Time)* - Starting Time) $\geq \Delta t$ (Predefined Time) or $T^*-T \geq \Delta t$

- Calculate $h(PW_{ia}) = CID_i \oplus h(d_i \oplus y \oplus t)$
- Calculate $Z_i = h(CID_i \oplus h(PW_{ia}))$ and validate $Y_i = h(t \oplus d_i \oplus Z_i \oplus y)$ equation, if confirm the remote server accept, otherwise reject the request and terminate the process.

2.4.4 Password Change Phase

User has the right to update the password of his or her smart-card freely and securely. The following steps are necessary for changing password.

- ✓ Insertion of smart card in the terminal (Smart Card contact machine)
- ✓ Enter old PW_{ia}
- ✓ Invitation for change of password request
- ✓ Choosing of new password PW_{ia}^*
- ✓ The terminal computations are: $d_i^* = d_i \oplus h(PW_{ia}) \oplus (PW_{ia}^*)$ which yields $h(PW_{ia}^*) \oplus h(x)$, d_i changed to d_i^* and user's password can also be changed easily.

2.4.5 Cryptanalysis of Das et al.'s Scheme

The cryptanalysis of Das et al.'s scheme shows password guessing attack and a deficiency of mutual authentication.

2.5 An's Scheme

An's [9] presented a new three-factor authentication scheme and enhanced the Das et al.'s [10] scheme. The enhanced Das et al.'s [10] scheme is divided by An's [9] into parts i.e. the registration phase, login and authentication phases.

Symbols and its Description			
U_a	User a	R_a	Trusted Registration center a
S_a	Server a	A_a	Attacker or Adversary

ID_a	Identity	B_a	Biometric
PW_{ia}	Password of the user i	$h(.)$	Hash function
X_s	Hidden evidence conserved by server	C_a	user center
m||n	Concatenation among m and n		
m⊕n	bitwise X-OR process among m and n		

Table- 4: Notations Used for An's Scheme

2.5.1 Registration Phase

The registration of a user U_a is necessary for before logging into the remote server so, whereas U_a represents user and R_a for trusted server. The following steps are performed in this phase:

I: User U_a submits Identity ID_a, password (PW_{ia}⊕K) and Biometric information (B_a⊕K) to a register server R_a via private channel.

II: R_a computes:

$$f_a = h(B_a \oplus K),$$

$$r_a = h(PW_{ia} \oplus K) \oplus f_a \text{ and}$$

$$e_a = h(ID_a \| X_s) \oplus r_a, \text{ where the Xs are secret value created by the server.}$$

III: R_a supplies (ID_a, h(.), f_a, e_a) arguments towards user's smart card and then to user through private path, user also store a random arbitrary number K into the memory of smart card.

C_a	R_a
ID_a, (PW_{ia}⊕K), (B_a⊕K) ⟶	
	Computations: $f_a = h(B_a \oplus K)$
	$r_a = (PW_{ia} \oplus K) \oplus f_a$
	$e_a = h(ID_a \| X_S) \oplus r_a$
⟵ {ID_a, h(.), f_a, e_a}	

to smart card along with K for storing, final arguments are {K, ID_a, h(.), f_a, e_a}

Registration Phase

2.5.2 Login Phase

Whenever C_a desires to login S_a, the user U_a has to be able to pass from the steps below.

1: User U_a provides smart card into a terminal for logging and scan biometrics B_a, the biometrics are $h(B_a \oplus K)$ and stored in f_a, so that U_a permits the biometrics proof.

2: Now user U_a provides the ID_a and PW_{ia}, the smart card calculates:
$r_a{'} = h(PW_{ia} \oplus K) \oplus f_a$, $\dot{M}_1 = e_a \oplus r_a{'}$, $\dot{M}_2 = \dot{M}_1 \oplus R_a$ and $\dot{M}_3 = h(\dot{M}_1 \| R_c)$.

3: The U_a directs the login request $\{ID_a, \dot{M}_2, \dot{M}_3\}$ to S_a.

2.5.3 Authentication Phase

1: The server (S_a) checks the format of identity (ID_a).

2: If the identity (ID_a) become legal, server (S_a) calculates $\dot{M}_4 = h(X_S \| ID_a)$ and $\dot{M}_5 = \dot{M}_2 \oplus \dot{M}_4$.

3: Server (S_a) verifies whether $\dot{M}_3 \stackrel{?}{=} h(\dot{M}_5)$ matches or not, if matched, the server (S_a) calculates:

$\dot{M}_6 = \dot{M}_4 \oplus R_S$,

$\dot{M}_7 = h(\dot{M}_2 \| \dot{M}_5)$ and

$\dot{M}_8 = h(R_S)$, where R_S is a secret digit created by the server.

4: Then, S_a directs $\{\dot{M}_6, \dot{M}_7, \dot{M}_8\}$ message to C_a.

5: Upon getting the answer message, U_a verifies $M_7 = h(M_2 \| R_C)$ or not. If same, U_a calculates $\dot{M}_9 = \dot{M}_6 \oplus \dot{M}_1$.

6: U_a verifies whether $M_8 = h(\dot{M}_9)$ or not. If matched, U_a calculates $\dot{M}_{10} = h(\dot{M}_6 \| \dot{M}_9)$.

7: Then, U_a directs the $\{\dot{M}_{10}\}$ message to S_a.

8: Upon receiving the message, S_a verifies $M_{10} = h(M_6 \| R_s)$ message. If matched, S_a receives the request.

C_a	S_a
Verifies $f_a = h(B_a \oplus K)$	
Provides ID_a and PW_{ia}	
Calculates	
$r_a{'} = h(PW_{ia} \oplus K) \oplus f_a$	
$\dot{M}_1 = e_a \oplus r_a{'}$	
$\dot{M}_2 = \dot{M}_1 \oplus R_C$	
$\dot{M}_3 = h(\dot{M}_1 \| R_C)$ $\xrightarrow{\{ID_a, \dot{M}_2, \dot{M}_3\}}$	
	Verifies ID_a
	Calculates $\dot{M}_4 = h(ID_a \| X_S)$
	$\dot{M}_5 = \dot{M}_2 \oplus \dot{M}_4$
	Verifies $\dot{M}_3 = h(\dot{M}_4 \| \dot{M}_5)$?

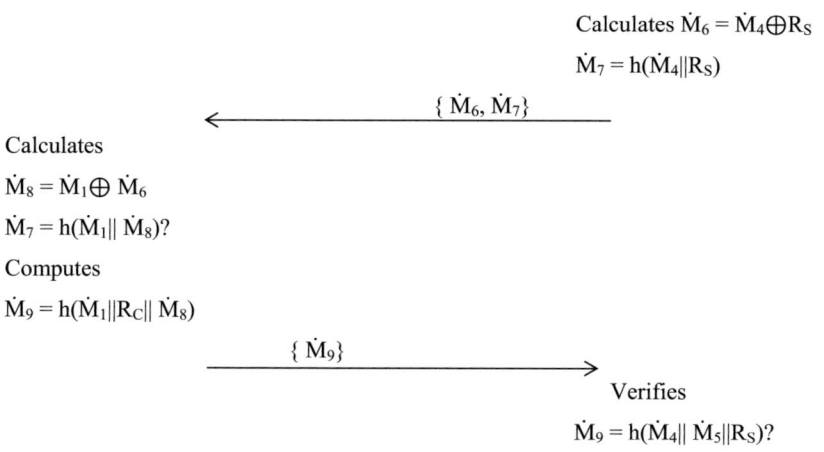

Login and Authentication Phases

2.5.4 Cryptanalysis of An's Scheme

The cryptanalysis of An's scheme shows many attacks i.e. it is vulnerable to replay, spoofing attacks, masquerade, impersonation and insider attacks. The scheme is also failing to offer mutual authentication.

2.6 Park et al.'s Scheme

Park et al.'s [7] proposed a scheme based on biometrics including smart card for authentication which is given below.

Symbols and its Description			
C_a	User a	R_a	A registration center a
S_a	Server a	A_a	Attacker a
ID_{ia}	Identity	B_a	Biometric Template of a
PW_{ia}	Password	$h(.)$	Hashing operation

Table- 5: Notations Used for Park et al.'s Scheme

2.6.1 Registration Phase

Suppose x and $PU_S = g^x$ represent server S_{ia} private key, a high entropy random integer g belongs to a set of integers Z_P is also used in the scheme for becoming more secure. The following computations are performed in this scheme:

(R1) User U_{ia} chooses a random number R_A, ID_{ia}, PW_{ia} and biometric B_a then computed: $DPW_{ia}=h(PW_{ia}\|R_A)$, $f_a=h(B_a\|R_A)$ and gives $\{ID_{ia}, DPW_{ia}, f_a\}$ to the remote registered server R_a through a private path.

(R2) The registry server R_a calculates $r_a = DPW_{ia} \oplus f_a$, $e_a = h(ID_{ia}\|x) \oplus r_a$ and store $\{h(.), f_a, PU_S, e_a\}$ in the memory of a smart card; whereas $PU_S = g^x$ is the public key of the server.

(R3) User U_{ia} at the moment also supply R_A towards smart card.

2.6.2 Login Phase

If the consumer desires to connect the remote server without any difficulty, the user U_{ia} has to pass from the following steps.

(L1) First of all insert smart card in the terminal, produce biometric for the verification of the user's biometrics B_a. If $h(B_a\|R_A)$ and the stored template are matched, the user U_{ia} permit the smart card for calculations.

(L2) Next the user input its ID_{ia}, PW_{ia} and smart card, creates a random number "a" and computes: $r_a = h(PW_{ia}\|R_A) \oplus s\, f_a$, $Y = e_a \oplus r_a$, $R_U = g^a$, $CID_{ia} = ID_{ia} \oplus R_{UA}$ and $MAC_1 = h(Y\|ID_{ia}\|R_{UA})$. Then sends $\{CID_{ia}, R_U, MAC_1\}$ request message to server S_a.

2.6.3 Authentication Phase

Whenever the server received the message $\{CID_{ia}, R_U, MAC_1\}$, the registered server has to complete the following steps:

(A1) $R_{UA} = R_U^x$, $ID_{ia} = CID_{ia} \oplus R_{UA}$ and $Y = h(ID_{ia}\|x)$. The server checked the right of MAC_1 by associating with $h(Y\|ID_{ia}\|R_{UA})$. If the validly is beyond the pre-defined schedule the server rejects the message and the authentication become stop, and if goes successfully, the server selects another random number "b" and calculate:

$$R_S = g^b$$
$$SK = R_U^b,$$
$$MAC_2 = h(SK\|R_U\|R_S)$$

And sends the replay message $\{R_S, MAC_2\}$ to the user U_a.

(A2) Once getting $\{R_S, MAC_2\}$ message from the server the U_{ia} check the authenticity of MAC_2 by associating with $h(R_S^a\|R_U\|R_S)$, if the session key is successful then validation of the message is occurring.

2.6.4 Cryptanalysis of Park et al.'s Scheme

The scheme was not mentioned that the forward confidentiality might be done by the assistance of asymmetric cryptography or at least two exponential functions happening on the server. Therefore, the scheme is failing to provide confidentiality.

2.7 Zhu-Xu-Feng's Scheme

Zhu-Xu-Feng's was presented a protocol [11] based on symmetric key cryptography to overcome some weaknesses of those schemes defined before for mutual authentication. Zhu-Xu-Feng's protocol [11] consists of the following phases:

Symbols	Descriptions		
• ID_i:	The user i's Identity	ID_j:	The user j's Identity
• PW_i:	The user i's Password	R_i:	random number
• T_i:	timestamp of i's	T_S:	timestamp of S's
• ΔT:	threshold of both systems	$h(.)$:	hash function
• $E_X(Y)$:	Y encrypted by session key X	$\oplus$:	bitwise function
• x mod p:	The residue of x divided by p	$\|$:	Concatenate function
• m and n:	prime numbers such that $m = 2n + 1$		
• Z_n^*:	multiplicative inverse of Z_n	Z_n:	Ring integer % n

Table- 6: Notations Used for Zhu-Xu-Feng's Scheme

2.7.1 Initial Phase

The remote system selects two big integer numbers, that is "m" and "n" such that $m = 2n+1$, selects a secret key of server "x" belongs to a set of integers (Z_n^*) and h(.), that is {set of 0 and 1}$^* \rightarrow Z_n^*$.

2.7.2 Registration Phase

The user provides ID_i and PW_i to a remote server via a private path. The server calculates $B = h(ID_i)^x + h(PW_i)\%p$ and stores $\{ID_i, B_i, h(.), m, n\}$ parameters in smart card memory.

2.7.3 Login Phase

The legitimate user provides smart card to a machine for logging and enters ID_i along with PW_i, smart card selects a digit "w" such that w∈ Z_n^*, sets timestamp/freshness T_i with the present time and calculates:

$B_1' = (B_1 - h(PW_i))^w \% p$, $W_1 = h(ID_i)^w \% p$ and $C_1 = h(T_i \| B_1' \| W_1 \| ID_i)$. Then the user transmits $\{ID_i, C_1, W_1, T_i\}$ to the remote server.

2.7.4 Authentication Phase

In this phase, first-of-all the server verify the identity and freshness T_i and compare by using the threshold values. The whole scenarios are explained by the following set of computations:

User	Server
2nd Phase	
Selects ID_i, PW_i $\{ID_i, PW_i\} \rightarrow$	$B_1 = h(ID_i)^x + h(PW_i) \% p$
$\leftarrow$ Smart Card	Store $\{ID_i, B_1, h(.), m, n\}$
3rd and 4th Phases	
Input ID_i, PW_i	
Choose $w \in Z_n^*$	
$B_1' = (B_1 - h(PW_i))^w \% p$	
$W_1 = h(ID_i)^w \% p$	
$C_1 = h(T_i \| B_1' \| W_1 \| ID_i)$	
$\{ID_i, C_1, W_1, T_i\} \rightarrow$	
	Verify ID_i, T_i
	$B_2 = (PW_i)^x \% p$
	$C_1 = h(T_i \| B_2 \| W_1 \| ID_i)?$
	Selects $w \in Z_n^*$
	$M_1 = h(ID_i)^w \% p$
	$C_2 = h(M_1 \| B_2 \| T_{ij} \| ID_i)$
$\leftarrow \{ID_i, C_1, M_1, T_{ij}\}$	
Verify ID_i, T_{ij}	
$C_1 = h(M_1 \| B_1 \| T_{ij} \| ID_i)?$	
$sk = h(ID_i \| M_1 \| W_1 \| (M_1)^w)$	$sk = h(ID_i \| M_1 \| W_1 \| (M_1)^w)$

Registration, Login and Authentication Phases

2.7.5 Cryptanalysis of Zhu-Xu-Feng's Scheme

The cryptanalysis of Zhu-Xu-Feng's scheme shows two weaknesses. First, it cannot resist masquerade attack and the second scheme is vulnerable to impersonation attack. Also the computation cost is maximized due to the reason that it completely in two-round trip, also shows counterfeit utilization of resources.

2.8 Song's Scheme

The scheme discussed above cannot resist impersonation attack because the ID_{ia} is independent of Biometric information. It is necessary that ID_{ia} must recover Biometric information. So a new scheme was presented by Ronggon Song [12] to overcome the security weaknesses in Zhu-Xu-Feng's [11] scheme, as discussed below:

Notations	Description
• ID_{ia}:	User a's Identity
• ID_{ib}:	User b's Identity
• PW_{ia}:	Password
• R_a:	Arbitrary number
• To:	Freshness or timestamp of the user
• TS:	Freshness or timestamp of server
• ΔT:	Threshold values of freshness
• $h(\cdot)$:	Hashing for secure information
• $E_X(P)$:	Encryption of P using X
• u mod v:	The limit of u divided by v
• $\oplus$:	XO-R function
• $\|$:	Concatenation function
• m and n:	Prime numbers m=2n+1;
• Z^*_n:	The multiplicative group Z_n;
• Z_n:	The jurisdiction of n;

Table- 7: Notation Used for Song's Scheme

2.8.1 Initialization Phase

First-of-all the Server selects a high entropy prime numerical value, that is m and n; and m=2n+1. Next selects a secret key "k" belongs to set of integers (Z^*_n) and h(.). Song's Scheme [12] is a symmetric based cryptographic functions with encryption and decryption operations that are represented by E(.) and D(.) respectively.

2.8.2 Registration Phase

The ID_{ia} (identity of user A) and password PW_{ia} are enter whenever insert the smart card into the machine by a user. Later the server received $\{ID_{ia}, PW_{ia}\}$, calculate $L_a = h(ID_{ia}\%p) \oplus h(PW_{ia})$ and stored $\{ID_{ia}, L_a, h(.), E(.)\}$ in the memory of a smart card.

2.8.3 Login Phase

In this phase, the owner of smart card enters his or her smart card into a machine and provides ID_{ia} & PW_{ia}. The smart card chooses a random integer number R_a, set the timestamp T_a for the freshness of the message and calculate $M_a = L_a \oplus h(PW_{ia})$, $O_a = E_{Xa}(R_a \oplus T_a)$ and $Q_a = h(T_a \| R_a \| O_a \| ID_{ia})$ Where E_{XA} is private key decipherment operation, the terminal then transmit $\{ID_{ia}, Q_a, O_a, T_a\}$ to the server for login request.

2.8.4 Authentication Phase

The remote peer/server first validate ID_{ia}, then PW_{ia} and the time interval T_a by matching $T^*-T_a \leq \Delta T$ with the predefined threshold time at the server, computes $M_a = h(ID_{ia}\%p)$ and $Z_a = D_{Xa}(PW_{ia}) \oplus T_a$ and check whether $h(T_a \| Z_a \| O_a \| ID_{ia})$ is equal to $h(ID_{ia} \| Z_a \| T_S)$, where T_S is the server up-to-date time, if so the authentication phase starts mutual authentication with the legal user.

User		Server
Select ID_{ia}, PW_{ia}	$\{ID_{ia}, PW_{ia}\}$ $\longrightarrow$	
		$B_a = h(ID^x_{ia}\%p) \oplus h(PW_{ia})$
This means Registration Phase $\longleftarrow$		
Store $\{ID_{ia}, B_a, h(.), E(.)\}$ into Smart Card		
Input ID_{ia}, PW_{ia} and Selects Z_a		
$M_a = L_a \oplus h(PW_{ia})$, $L^*_a = (L_a - h(PW_{ia}))^w \% p$		
$O_a = E_{Xa}(Z_a \oplus T_a)$		
$Q_a = h(T_a \| Z'_a \| O_a \| ID_{ia})$	$\{ID_{ia}, Q_a, O_a, T_a\}$ $\longrightarrow$	
		Verify ID_{ia}, T_a
		$M_a = h(ID^x_{ia}\%p)$
		$Z'_a = D_{Xa}(PW_{ia}) \oplus T_a$
		$Q_a ?= h(T_a \| Z'_a \| O_a \| ID_{ia})$
	$\longleftarrow \{ID_{ia}, Q_S, T_S\}$	$Q_S = h(ID_{ia} \| Z'_a \| T_S)$
Confirm ID_{ia}, T_S and verify $Q_S ?= h(ID_{ia} \| Z'_a \| T_S)$		

$sk = h(ID_{ia} || Z'_a || T_S || T_a)$ $\longleftrightarrow$ $sk = h(ID_{ia} || Z'_a || T_S || T_a)$

Registration, Login and Authentication

2.8.5 Cryptanalysis of Song's Scheme

The cryptanalysis of the Song's scheme [12] shows three weaknesses: first the scheme cannot resists insider attack, second the scheme has completed in multiple round trip, which shows counterfeit utilization of resources and third suffered from server spoofing attack.

2.9 Wu et al.'s Scheme [19]

It is also a three-factor authentication scheme, consists of five phases, i.e. initial, registration, login, authentication and password change phases, discuss below in detail:

Symbols and its Description			
U_i	User	S	server
ID_i	user Identity	ID_S	server Identity
PW_i	user password	x	server private key
B_i	user biometric	Q_S	server public key
L's	length parameter	$\oplus$	X-OR, bitwise operation
$h(.), h_1(.)$	one-way hash functions, i.e. range from 0 to 1 and {zero, one}$^{l's}$		
sk_u, sk_S	the session key established between user and server		
$E_X(.), D_X(.)$	encryption, decryption algorithms with private key X		

Table- 8: Notations used by Wu et al.'s Protocol

2.9.1 Initialization Phase

The remote server selects the fixed repeated tally set G produced by argument P through a big prime number n over a determinate area F_P on a curve. Then the remote server chooses x as secret key, store it and broadcasts $E(F_P)$, G, P.

2.9.2 Registration Phase

The user U_i performed the below steps:
1. First-of-all chooses ID_i, PW_i and a nonce r_i, trajectories B_i and gets $(R_{bi}, P_{bi}) = Gen(B_i)$, submits ID_i, $H_i = h(PW_i||R_{bi}) \oplus r_i$ to the remote server.
2. The remote server chooses a number e_i, calculates $B_1^* = h(ID_s||x||e_i) \oplus H_i \oplus h(ID_i||e_i)$ and $B_2^* = h(ID_i||x) \oplus H_i$ and relays B_1^*, B_2^*, P and e_i to the legitimate user.

3. The legitimate user calculates $B_1 = B_1^* \oplus r_i$ and $B_2 = B_2^* \oplus r_i$ and stores B_1, B_2, P, P_{bi} and e_i into cell phone device.

2.9.3 Login & Authentication Phases

The legitimate user provides ID_i, PW_i, B_i^* on the client side.
The cell phone chooses a number $\alpha \in Z_n^*$ and u_i, calculates $R_{bi} = Rep(B_i^*, P_{bi})$,
$C_1 = \alpha P$, $C_2 = B_1 \oplus h(PW_i \| R_{bi}) \oplus h(ID_i \| e_i) \oplus u_i$
$C_3 = B_2 \oplus h(PW_i \| R_{bi})$, $C_4 = h(C_1 \| C_2 \| C_3 \| e_i \| u_i)$ and $C_5 = E_{ui}(ID_i \| C_4)$

User U_i	Server S
Input ID_i, PW_i, B_i^*	
Generate $\alpha \in Z_n^*$, u_i	
Compute: $R_{bi} = Rep(B_i^*, P_{bi})$	
$C_1 = \alpha P$	
$C_2 = B_1 \oplus h(PW_i \| R_{bi}) \oplus h(ID_i \| e_i) \oplus u_i$	
$C_3 = B_2 \oplus h(PW_i \| R_{bi})$	
$C_4 = h(C_1 \| C_2 \| e_i \| u_i)$	
$C_5 = E_{ui}(ID_i \| C_4)$	
$\xrightarrow{m_1 = \{C_1, C_2, C_5, r_i\}}$	
	Compute $u_i' = h(ID_S \| x \| e_i) \oplus C_2$
	Decrypt C_5 and get ID_i', C_4'
	Compute $C_3' = h(ID_i' \| x)$
	Check $C_4'\ ?= h(C_1 \| C_2' \| C_3' \| e_i' \| u_i')$
	Choose $\beta \in Z_n^*$, $\bar{e}_i$
	Compute: $C_6 = h(ID_S \| x \| \bar{e}_i \|) \oplus h(ID_i' \| x)$
	$C_7 = \beta P$
	$C_8 = C_2' \oplus e_i \oplus \bar{e}_i$
	$C_9 = h(ID_i' \| x) \oplus u_i'$
	$sk_S = h_1(C_1 \| C_7 \| \beta C_1)$
	$C_{10} = h(ID_i' \| ID_S \| C_6 \| C_8 \| C_9 \| sk_S \| \bar{e}_i$
	$C_{11} = E_{C_9}(C_6 \| C_8 \| C_{10})$
$\xleftarrow{m_2 = \{C_7, C_{11}\}}$	
Compute $C_9' = C_3 \oplus u_i$	
Decrypt C_{11} and get C_6', C_8', C_{10}'	
Compute: $\bar{e}_i = C_8' \oplus C_2 \oplus e_i$	
$sk_u = h_1(C_1 \| C_7 \| \alpha C_7)$	

Check $C_{10}{'}$? = $h(ID_i\|ID_S\|C_6{'}\|C_8{'}\|C_9{'}\|sk_u\|\bar{e}_i)$

Compute $e_i{}^{new} = \bar{e}_i$, $B_1{}^{new} = C_6{'} \oplus C_3 \oplus h(PW_i\|R_{bi}) \oplus h(ID_i\|e_i{}^{new})$

Replace e_i, B_1 with $e_i{}^{new}$, $B_1{}^{new}$ respectively

Login & Authentication Phases of Wu et al.'s Scheme

2.9.4 Password or Biometrics Change Phase

The legitimate user can change his or her password or biometrics by using the following two steps.

1. The legitimate user U_i calculates the second phase and relays a request message for changing of password to the remote server. The remote server execute $S_a = h(u_i\|e_i\|C_3{'}\|C_2\|C_1)$ and transmit S_a.

2. After receving S_a checks it for correctness, i.e. S_a? = $h(u_i\|e_i\|C_3\|C_2\|C_1)$. If valid the legitimate user provides the fresh password $PW_i{}^{new}$ and fresh biometrics $B_i{}^{new}$ at that time. The cell phone calculates $R_{bi}{}^{new}$, $P_{bi}{}^{new}$) = Gen($B_i{}^{new}$), $B_1{}^{new} = B_1 \oplus h(PW_i\|R_{bi})$ $\oplus h(PW_i{}^{new}\|R_{bi}{}^{new})$ and $B_2{}^{new} = B_2 \oplus h(PW_i\|R_{bi}) \oplus h(PW_i{}^{new}\|R_{bi}{}^{new})$. So changes B_1, B_2, P_{bi} with $B_1{}^{new}$, $B_2{}^{new}$, $P_{bi}{}^{new}$

2.9.5 Cryptanalysis of Wu et al.'s Scheme

The protocol presented by Wu et al.'s [19] above have many drawbacks that are as follows:

i. In the registration phase it suffers from impersonation attack
ii. In the login phase it suffers from an offline PW_i guessing attack
iii. While in the change of password phase it suffer from an offline PW_i guessing attack
iv. Also doesn't provide re-registration and revocation facilities for the user

Therefore, Wu et al.'s protocol [19] failed for practical application.

2.10 Lee et al.'s Scheme

Lee et al.'s [13] proposed a scenario based on self-motivated identity for authentication of information at the remote server with smart card. In this scheme three main entities were used; user, provider and server. The whole scenario of the scheme includes four phases. These phases are described on by one under the following headings.

Symbols and its Description			
U_a	user	S_a	Server
RC	Cipher registrations	ID_{ia}	user identity
PW_{ia}	Password	m	secret number
x	stealthy key	CID_a	dynamic identity
sk	session key	$\|$	concatenation function
$\Rightarrow$	public channel	$\rightarrow$	private channel
$\oplus$	XO-R function	T_i	freshness or Timestamp

Table- 9: Notations Used for Lee et al.'s Scheme

2.10.1 Registration Phase

R1: $U_{ia} \Rightarrow RC$: The U_a selects ID_{ia} and PW_{ia} and a high entropy integer numbers m, calculates $h(m\|PW_{ia})$ and submits to the RC via private channel.

R2: RC calculates: $T_i = h(ID_{ia}\|x)$, $V_1 = T_i \oplus h(ID_{ia}\|h(m \oplus PW_{ia}))$, $B_1 = h(h(m \oplus PW_{ia})\|h(x\|y))$ and $H_1 = h(y_i)$.

R3: $RC \Rightarrow U_a$: The RC pic $(V_1, B_1, H_1, h(.), h(y))$ into U_a via private channel as shown below:

User U_a	Server S_a

The legitimate user knows ID_{ia}, PW_{ia}, $h(m \oplus PW_i)$

$\{ID_{ia}, PW_{ia}, h(m \oplus PW_{ia})\} \rightarrow$

Computes $T_i = h(ID_{ia}\|x)$, $H_1 = h(T_i)$

$V_1 = T_i \oplus h(ID_{ia}\|h(m \oplus PW_{ia}))$

$B_1 = h(h(m \oplus PW_{ia})\|h(x\|y))$

Store $(V_1, B_1, H_1, h(.), h(y))$

$\leftarrow$

Stored in the memory of a smart card along with me

The Registration Phase

2.10.2 Login & Authentication Phases

The user U_a provide idea into the legal server S_j along with a password, the following computations are performed in this phase:

L1: $T_i = V_1 \oplus h(ID_{ia} \| h(m \oplus PW_{ia}))$, $H_1' = h(T_i)$ and verify $H_1 ?= H_1'$ for equality, if equal it means that the message arrives from the legal user U_a.

L2: Smart card creates nonce and calculates:
$A_1 = h(T_i \| h(y) \| N_i)$, $P_{ab} = T_i \oplus h(h(y) \| N_i \| SID_b)$, $CID_a = h(m \oplus PW_{ia}) \oplus h(T_i \| A_1 \| N_i)$ and $Q_1 = h(B_1 \| A_1 \| N_i)$.

L3: $U_a \rightarrow S_b$: $\{Q_1, N_i, P_{ab}, CID_b\}$ message relays /pickup by the user from the remote server as shown below:

User U_a	Server S_a
$T_i = V_1 \oplus h(ID_{ia} \| h((m \oplus PW_{ia}))$	
$H_1' = h(T_i)$ and Generate N_i	
$A_1 = h(T_i \| h(y) \| N_i)$	
$CID_a = h(m \oplus PW_{ia}) \oplus h(T_i \| A_1 \| N_i)$	
$P_{ab} = T_i \oplus h(h(y) \| N_i \| SID_b)$	
$Q_1 = h(B_1 \| A_1 \| N_i)$ Store $(CID_a, P_{ab}, Q_1, N_i)$ →	
	Calculates $T_i = P_1 \oplus h(y) \| N_i \| SID_b)$
	$A_1 = h(T_i \| h(y) \| N_i)$
	$h(m \oplus PW_{ia}) = CID_a \oplus h(T_i \| A_1 \| N_i)$
	$B_1 = h(h(m \oplus PW_{ia}) \| h(x \| y))$
	$Q_1' = h(B_1 \| A_1 \| N_i)$, $M_{ab} = h(B_1 \| N_j \| A_1 \| SID_b)$
← Generate (M_{ab}, N_j)	
$M'_{ab} = h(B_1 \| N_j \| A_1 \| SID_b)$	
$M''_{ab} = h(B_1 \| N_j \| A_1 \| SID_j)$	
Generate M''_{ab} →	
	$M''_{ab} = h(B_1 \| N_j \| A_1 \| CID_b)$
Generate $sk = h(B_1 \| N_i \| N_j \| A_1 \| CID_b)$	

Login and Authentication Phases

2.10.3 Password Change Phase

The legitimate user inserts her smart card in the card readable machine to facilitate the owner by changing ID_{ia} and PW_{ia} easily, freely and securely. The following operations are accomplished:

User	RC
User Knows (ID_{ia}, PW_{ia})	$(V_1, B_1, H_1, m, h(.), h(y))$
Input ID_{ia}, PW_{ia}	
$T_i = V_1 \oplus h(ID_{ia}\|h((m \oplus PW_{ia}))$	
$H_1 = h(T_i)$	
Checks $H_1' = H_1$ if yes selects $(PW_{ia})_{new}$ and m_{new}	
Compute $h(m_{new} \oplus (PW_{ia})_{new})$ and $V_{new} = T_i \oplus h(ID_{ia}\|h(m_{new} \oplus (PW_{ia})_{new}))$	
Generate $(ID_{ia}, h(m_{new} \oplus (PW_{ia})_{new}))$ $\longrightarrow$	
	Calculates $(B_1)_{new} = h(h(m_{new} \oplus (PW_{ia})_{new})\|h(x\|y))$
	$\longleftarrow$ Generate $\{(B_1)_{new}\}$
Changes the values V_1 and B_1 with $(V_1)_{new}$ and $(B_1)_{new}$	
Password Change Phase	

2.10.4 Cryptanalysis of Lee et al.'s Scheme

The scheme is failing due to the following points

1. The attacker can effortlessly capture the channel message and insert, delete, update or modify it because the channel is totally under the control of the attacker.

2. Also the attacker might either get the secret or draw the conceals in smart cards

2.11 Lue et al.'s Scheme

Lue et al.'s [14] crypt-analyzed the Lee et al.'s scheme and proposed a new scheme based on symmetric key primitives using smart cards. Lue et al.'s [14] shows three main weaknesses in Lee et al.'s scheme that is masquerade attack, offline password guessing attack and server spoofing attack. Therefore, to overcome these drawbacks they presented an effective and robust authentication scheme consists of three entities (user, server and terminal) and four steps. These are described one-by-one under the following headings.

Symbols and its Description

U_a	User	S_a	Server
RC	Registrations	ID_{ia}	Identity
PW_{ia}	User password	m	Secret number
X	Secret key	N, m	A random number
CID_a	Dynamic identity	sk	Session key
$\Rightarrow$	Private channel	$\rightarrow$	Public channel
$\oplus$	X-OR Function	$\parallel$	Concatenate-function

Table- 10: Notations Used for Lue et al.'s Scheme

2.11.1 Registration Phase

I: $U_a \Rightarrow RC$: ID_{ia}, $h(m \oplus PW_{ia}) = A_1$ and submitting it to the server by a private channel.

II: By getting parameters from the server, RC chooses an integer number R_1 and computes:

$T_i = h(R_1 \parallel x)$,

$Z_1 = R_1 \oplus ID_1 h(b \oplus PW_{ia}) \parallel h(m \oplus PW_{ia})$,

$V_1 = T_i \oplus (ID_{ia} \oplus \parallel h(m \oplus PW_{ia}))$,

$B_1 = h(b \oplus PW_{ia}) \oplus ID_{ia} \oplus h(h(m \oplus PW_{ia} \oplus R_1) \parallel h(x \parallel y))$ and $H_1 = h(T_1)$.

III: $RC \Rightarrow U_a$: The server issues (Z_1, v_1, B_1, H_1, b, h(.) and h(y)) to the card's memory as shown

User	RC

ID_{ia}, PW_{ia} chooses m and calculates $A_1 = h(m \oplus PW_{ia})$

$\xrightarrow{\text{Sends } \{ID_{ia}, A_1\}}$

The RC calculates

$T_1 = h(R_1 \parallel x)$

$Z_1 = R_1 \oplus ID_{ia} \oplus h(m \oplus PW_{ia})$

$V_1 = T_1 \oplus h(ID_{ia} \parallel h(m \oplus PW_{ia}))$

$B_1 = h(m \oplus PW_{ia}) \oplus ID_{ia} \oplus h(h(m \oplus PW_{ia} \oplus R_1 \| h(x\|y))$

$H_1 = h(T_1)$ and

Stores $\{Z_1, V_1, B_1, H_1, h(.), h(y)\}$ into the smart card

All the entries in the smart card are hashed $h(.)$.

The Registration Phase

2.11.2 Login & Verification Phases

The legitimate user provides ID_i, PW_i on demand, the following steps are performed in this phase of Lue et al.'s scheme.

L1: The smart card then calculates $R_1 = Z_1 \oplus ID_{ia} \oplus h(m \oplus PW_{ia})$, $T_i = V_1 \oplus h(ID_{ia} \oplus \| h(m \oplus PW_{ia})$ and $H_1' = h(T_i)$ and verify it H_1? $= H_1$, if equal then further processing continues, otherwise rejects and termination of the process.

L2: The card produces a random number N_i and computes:
$O_1 = h(m \oplus PW_{ia}) \oplus ID_{ia}$, $B_1 = h(h(m \oplus PW_{ia} \oplus R_1) \| h(x\|y))$, $A_1 = h(T_i \| h(y) \| N_i))$, $CID_a = h(m \oplus PW_{ia} \oplus R_1) \oplus h(T_i \oplus \| A_1 \| N_i)$, $P_{ab} = T_i \oplus h(h(y) \| N_i \| SID_b)$ and $Q_1 = h(O_1 \| A_1 \| N_i)$ as shown below:

User	Server
$ID_{ia}, PW_{ia}, h(b \oplus PW_{ia})$ →	
	$T = h(ID_{ia}\|x)$
	$V = T \oplus h(ID_{ia} \| h(b \oplus PW_{ia}))$
	$B = h(h(b \oplus PW_{ia}) \| h(x\|y))$
	$H = h(T)$
	← Store $(V, B, H, h(.), h(y))$
$T = V \oplus h(ID \| h((b \oplus PW_{ia}))$	
$H = h(T)$	
Generate N	
$A = h(T \| h(y) \| N)$	
$CID_{ia} = h(b \oplus PW_{ia}) \oplus h(T\|A\|N)$	
$P = T \oplus h(h(y) \| N \| SID_{ia})$	
$Q = h(B\|A\|N)$ Store (CID_{ia}, P, Q, N) →	
	$T = P \oplus h(y) \| N \| SID_{ia})$

$A = h(T\|h(y)\|N)$

$h(b \oplus PW_{ia}) = CID_{ia} \oplus h(T\|A\|N)$

$B = h(h(b \oplus PW_{ia})\|h(x\|y))$

$Q = h(B\|A\|N)$

$M = h(B\|N\|A\|SID_{ia})$

← Generate (M, N)

$M = h(B\|N\|A\|SID)$
$M' = h(B\|N\|A\|SID)$

Generate M' →

$M' = h(B\|N\|A\|CID)$

← Generate SK = $h(B\|N\|A\|CID)$ →

The Login and Verification Phases

2.11.3 Password Change Phase

In this phase the following calculations are performed:

P1: Insertion of smart card and provide ID_{ia} and PW_{ia}

P2: The smart card computes $V_1 \oplus h(ID_{ia}\|h(m \oplus PW_{ia}))$ and obtained T_i^* and calculate $H_1^* = h(T_i^*)$ and compare with H_1. If verify, then proceed $R_1 = Z_1 \oplus ID_{ia} \oplus h(m \oplus PW_{ia})$ and request for a new password

$(Z_1)_{new} = R_1 \oplus ID_{ia} \oplus h(m_{new} \oplus (PW_{ia})_{new})$ and

$(V_1)_{new} = T_i \oplus h(ID_{ia}\|h(m_{new} \oplus \oplus (PW_{ia})_{new}))$ and finally the Z_i, V_i, B_i with $(Z_1)_{new}, (V_1)_{new}$ and $(B_1)_{new}$.

2.11.4 Cryptanalysis of Lue et al Scheme

The scheme is suffering from traceability attack, therefore, failed to authenticate the legal user or server, due to anonymity problem.

2.12 Tsai et al.'s Scheme [25]

This section illustrates the working and review analysis of Tsai et al. scheme as follows:

2.12.1 Working of Tsai et al. scheme

Tsai et al.'s scheme [25] consists of three levels: The Registration, The Login and The Authentication phase. The notations that have been used in their scenarios are given as under.

Notations	Descriptions
Ui	ith user
IDi, PWi	Identity and Password of user U_i
PID_j	The shared value between RC and Sj
x, y	RC's master secret key and random secret key
S_j	The jth server
SID_j, R_j	The identity of Sj, Shared secret between Sj and RC
$T_n(.)$	Chebyshev polynomial of degree n
q	Temporary secret key
h(.)	A secure hash digests function
‖	Concatenate function
⊕	XOR function

Table- 11: Notation used for Tsai et al.'s Scheme

2.12.2 The Server Registration Phase

The Tsai et al. scheme consists of one trusted RC and n number of trusted servers Sj, where j=1…..n. The Sj is already registered with RC by sharing a secret Rj between both of the entities (RC and Sj) using a secure channel. Initially, the server Sj sends its identity SIDj to RC. RC, then, computes Rj= h(s, SIDj), and sends it to Sj over a private channel.

2.12.3 The User Registration Phase

The Ui gets registered with RC, while, Sj has already been registered with RC. Afterwards Ui can access all Sj servers, registered with the same RC. The Ui gets registered with RC in the following manner:

1. The Ui chooses IDi and PWi. Next, it creates random digit n and sends {ID_i, h(IDi, PWi, n)} to RC.

2. RC computes PIDi = (IDi, r)⊕ h(s), Ri=h(IDi, s) ⊕h(IDi, PWi, n) and stores {PIDi, Ri, h()} in a smart card. Next, it sends the SC to Ui.

3. Ui receives, and inserts n additionally in a smart card.

2.12.4 The Login and Authentication Phase

1. On this phase the Ui computes $h(IDi \parallel s) = Ri \oplus h(IDi, PWi, n)$, $q = h(h(ID, s), PIDi, SIDj)$, $C_1 = h(PIDi, SIDj, h(IDi, s)) \oplus T_a(q)$, and $M_1 = h(PIDi, SIDj, h(IDi, s), T_a(q))$. Next, it sends the message $\{PIDi, SIDj, C_1, M_1\}$ to Sj.

2. The Sj receives $\{PIDi, SIDj, C_1, M_1\}$ and computes $M_2 = h(PIDi, SIDj, C_1, M_1, Rj)$, and sends the message $\{PIDi, SIDj, C_1, M_1, M_2\}$ to RC for further verification.

3. The RC receives the message $\{PIDi, SIDj, C_1, M_1, M_2\}$ and computes $(IDi, r) = PIDi \oplus h(s)$, $h(IDi, s)$, $q = h(h(ID, s), PIDi, SIDj)$, $T_a(q) = h(PIDi, SIDj, h(IDi, s)) \oplus C_1$, $Rj = h(SIDj, s)$, $M_1 = h(PIDi, SIDj, h(IDi, s), T_a(q))$, and $M_2 = h(PIDi, SIDj, C_1, M_1, Rj)$. Next, it compares the equation equality $M_1'\ ?= M_1$, $M_2'\ ?= M_2$. If true, then further computes $PIDi' = (IDi, r') \oplus h(s)$, $M_3 = (IDi, q, T_a(q)) \oplus h(SIDj, Rj, PIDi, M_1, M_2)$, $M_4 = PIDi' \oplus h(h(ID, s), PIDi, IDi)$, $M_5 = h(SIDj, IDi, Rj, q, M_3, M_4)$, and finally sends the message $\{M_3, M_4, M_5\}$ to Sj for verification.

4. The Sj computes $(IDi, g, T_a(q)) = M_3 \oplus h(SIDj, Rj, PIDi, M_1, M_2)$, $M_5' = h(SIDj, IDi, Rj, q, M_3, M_4)$, and compares the values $M_5'\ ?= M_5$. If successful, then compute $M_6 = q \oplus T_b(q)$, $SKj = h(T_{ba}(q))$, $M_7 = h(SKj, q, T_b(q), M_4, M_6)$, and sends the message $\{M_4, M_6, M_7\}$ to Ui for verification.

5. The Ui, receives the message $\{M_4, M_6, M_7\}$, and computes $PIDi' = M_4 \oplus h(h(ID, s), PIDi, IDi)$, $T_b(q) = q \oplus M_6$, $SKi = h(T_{ab}(q))$, $M_7' = h(SKi, q, T_b(q), M_4, M_6)$. It then compares $M_7'\ ?= M_7$. If found true, computes $M_8 = h(PIDi, Ski, q, M_4, T_b(q))$, and sends $\{M_8\}$ to Sj for final verification.

6. The Sj computes $M_8' = h(PIDi, Skj, q, M_4, T_b(q))$, and matches the equality $M_8'\ ?= M_8$. If this comes true, then it establishes the final session key as $Ski = SKj = h(T_{ab}(q)) = h(T_{ba}(q))$.

2.12.5 Cryptanalysis of Tsai et al. Scheme

The Tsai et al.'s scenario is a multi-server verification protocol based on CCM (Chebyshev Chaotic Map). Although, the scheme has been well-formulated, despite, the scheme is defenseless to server-spoofing and guessing of password attack, subject to the lifted smart card. Suppose an opponent A finds the SC, steal its contents, and places the card at the right place without the user's knowledge. Next, if A comes to know the user's ID through any social engineering tactics, then it may launch the server-spoofing attack successfully. As far cryptanalysis, suppose, an attacker approaches the public messages, i.e., PID_i, PID_i' and $M_4 = PID_i' \oplus h(h(ID, s), PID_i, ID_i)$ from two successive sessions.

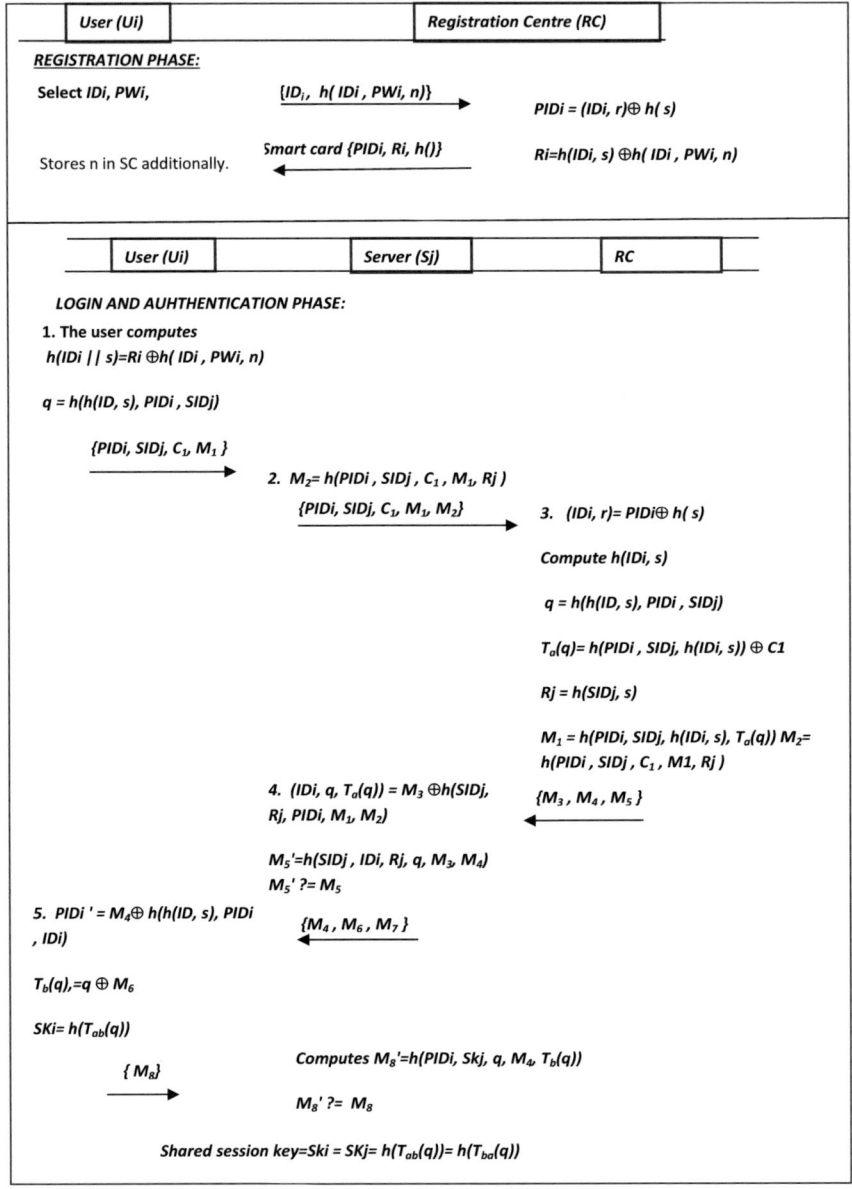

Tsai et al. Model all phases

Next, it derives h(h(ID, s), PIDi , IDi) by computing PIDi' $\oplus$ M_4. Next, it employs the stolen card contents and tries all combinations of password PWi by computing and checking (7) and (8).

$$h(IDi , s)^* = Ri \oplus h(IDi \| PWi^* \| b) \qquad (7)$$

$$h\,(h(IDi , s)^* \| PIDi \| IDi)\ ?= h(h(ID, s), PIDi , IDi) \qquad (8)$$

If any of the guessed passwords PWi^* hit, the adversary comes up with the right h(IDi , s) parameter. Next, it may launch the server-spoofing attack by constructing the $\{M_4 , M_6 , M_7 \}$ message successfully using the following steps.

1. It constructs M_4 by taking PIDi from Request message and constructing M_4 = $PIDi^{old}$ $\oplus$ h(h(ID, s), PIDi , IDi). As an advisory cannot generate a new PIDi, hence for generating M_4, it shall utilize an old value of PID_i^{old}. A user does not maintain the record of PIDi, so it cannot trace the replay of PID_i.
2. An attacker generates M_6 = q $\oplus$ $T_b(q)$, by constructing q = h(h(ID, s), PIDi , SIDj) and $T_b(q)$, assuming a random number b.
3. Next, A generates M_7 = h(SKj, q, $T_b(q)$, M_4 ,M_6) by constructing SKj = $T_{ba}(q)$.
4. In this manner it may send the message $\{M_4 , M_6 , M_7 \}$ to Ui without failure, and the user gets deceived with the establishment of session key as SKj = $T_{ab}(q)$.

2.13 Wu-Xu-Xiong Scheme

This scheme is working for both wired and wireless communication channels. They presented that their scheme is designed for client/server manner. Their scheme catches the ideas of discrete logarithm problem, consists of five phases: the registration, login, authentication, change of Password and card revocation. The review is as under:

Notations or Preliminaries			
1. S, ID_s:	the remote server and its Identity	2. U_i, ID_i:	The user and its Identity
3. p, q:	Large Prime numbers	4. g:	Multiplicative group generator
5. x:	secrete key	6. PW_i:	Password of User U_i
7. r_i, α, β:	Random Numbers	8. $\Rightarrow$	A Secure Channel
9. SK_u, SK_s:	session keys	10. h(.):	hashing
11. l:	parameters	12: A:	An Adversary
13. $\rightarrow$:	An insecure path	14: a? = b:	Whether a equal to b

Table- 12: Notations used in Wu-Xu-Xiong Scheme

2.13.1 Registration Phase

The remote server chooses two high-scale prime numbers m and n everywhere it is $m = 2n + 1$. Small q is multiplicative group G in the direction of n. The remote server also selects a controlling key x and $h(.)$, $h_1(.) : \{0, 1\}^* \rightarrow \{0, 1\}^l$. The following steps are performed in the registration phase:

(1) $U_i \Rightarrow S: ID_i, HPW_i$

It means that U_i selects identity, password and random integer b_i, calculate $HPW_i = h(PW_i\|b_i)$, and the relays to the server over a secure channel.

(2) $S \Rightarrow U_i$ smart card

Registration is done only once, at the time when someone demanded for a smart card. In this stage the owner inserts a smart card in the machine and choose a big integer N_i and random integer a_i, computes

$B_1 = h(x\|a_i) \oplus h(ID_i\|HPW_i)$

$B_2 = h(ID_i\|x\|N_i) \oplus HPW_i$

And the values in the memory of the database on the remote server and B_1, B_2, g, p, h (.) into the memory of a smart card.

(3) $U_i \Rightarrow$ card: B_3

At this step of the registration phase legitimate user computes $B_3 = h(ID_i\|PW_i) \oplus b_i$ and also stores in the smart card memory and issue it to the user to whom demanded for it.

2.13.2 Login and Authentication Phases

First-of-all U_i provides smart-card in the machine and given ID_i along with PW_i then calculates:

$b_i' = h(ID_i\|PW_{ia}) \oplus B_3$. The card generates two high entropy random numbers r_i and $\alpha \in [1, q-1]$ and calculates $HPW_{ia} = h(PW_{ia}\|b_i)$, $R_i' = B_1 \oplus r_i$, $C_1 = h(ID_i\|HPW_{ia}) \oplus r_i$, $C_2 = g^\alpha \% P$, $k_i = B_2 \oplus HPW_{ia}$ and $C_3 = h(ID_i\|C_2\|k_i\|r_i\|a_i)$ then $S \rightarrow U_i : M_1$ etc. The phases of Wu et al.'s scheme [21] is shown below:

User U_i Computing	Server S Computation

Login:

Inputs ID_i with PW_i

Computes $b_i = h(ID_i\|PW_i) \oplus B_3$

Generates r_i and α and computes:

$HPW_i = h(PW_i\|b_i')$

$R_i = B_1 \oplus r_i$,

$C_1 = h(ID_i\|HPW_i) \oplus r_i$

$C_2 = g^\alpha \% P$

$k_i = B_2 \oplus HPW_i$

$C_3 = h(ID_i\|C_2\|k_i\|r_i\|a_i)$

$\qquad\qquad M_1 = \{R_i, a_i, E_{C1}(ID_i\|C_2\|C_3\|r_i)\} \rightarrow$

Authentication:

$\qquad\qquad\qquad$ Computes $C_1' = h(x\|a_i) \oplus R_i$

$\qquad\qquad\qquad$ Decrypts $E_{C1}(ID_i\|C_2\|C_3\|r_i)$ with C_1', and get ID_i', C_2', C_3' and r_i'

$\qquad\qquad\qquad$ Checks the memory for ID_i' and the nonce N_i

$\qquad\qquad\qquad$ Computes $k_i' = h(ID_i'\|x\|N_i)$

$\qquad\qquad\qquad$ Checks $C_3' \stackrel{?}{=} h(ID_i'\|C_2'\|k_i'\|r_i'\|a_i)$

$\qquad\qquad\qquad$ Generate β and a_i', computes:

$\qquad\qquad\qquad$ $C_4 = g^\beta \bmod p$, $C_5 = (C_2')^\beta \bmod p$

$\qquad\qquad\qquad$ $C_6 = k_i \oplus h(r_i')$, $C_7 = h(x\|a_i')$

$\qquad\qquad\qquad$ $sk_s = h_1(ID_i'\|C_1'\|C_2'\|C_4\|C_5\|k_i')$

$\qquad\qquad\qquad$ $C_8 = h_1(ID_i'\|C_1'\|C_2'\|C_4\|C_5\|C_6\|C_7\|sk_s\|a_i')$

$\qquad\qquad \leftarrow M_2 = \{E_{C6}(C_4\|C_7\|C_8\|a_i')\}$

Computes $C_6' = k_i \oplus h(r_i)$

Decrypt the message and get C_4', C_7', C_8' and a_i''

Computes:

$C_5' = (C_4')^\alpha \bmod p$

$Sk_u = h_1(ID_i\|C_1\|C_2\|C_4'\|C_5'\|k_i)$

$C_8'' = h(ID_i\|C_1\|C_2\|C_4'\|C_5'\|C_6'\|C_7'\|sk_u\|a_i'')$

Checks $C_8' \stackrel{?}{=} C_8''$

Computes:

$B_1' = h(ID_i\|h(PW_i\|b_i')) \oplus C_7'$

Replace B_1 and a_i with B_1' and a_i''

Login and Authentication Phases

2.13.3 Password Change Phase

Whenever the U_i desires to change his or her password, provide ID_i and PW_i, the following steps are performed:

1. After sending the message M_1 to the server, a change of password demand also sends. First Ui become authenticated and then relays $C_9 = h(ID_i\|C'_1\|C'_2\|k'_i\|r'_i\|a_i)$ and request for permission.
2. If $C_9 = h(ID_i\|C_1\|C_2\|k_i\|r_i\|a_i)$ passed by the user, then enter a new password message is displayed PW_i^{new}. At this stage the smart card chooses a random number b_i^{new} and computes:

$$B_1^{new} = B_1 \oplus h(ID_i\|h(PW_i\|b'_i)) \oplus h(ID_i\|(PW_i^{new}\|b_i^{new}))$$
$$B_2^{new} = B_2 \oplus h(PW_i\|b'_i) \oplus h(PW_i^{new}\|b_i^{new})$$
$$B_3^{new} = h(ID_i\|PW_i^{new}) \oplus b_i^{new}$$

3. The values of B_1, B_2 and B_3 replaced by B_1^{new}, B_2^{new} and B_3^{new}.

2.13.4 Card Revocation Phase

The legitimate user U_i after losing smart card, can easily demand from another by means of some credentials like $N_i^{new} = N_i+1$ and stored $\{ID_i, N_i^{new}\}$ in the database of smart card and the owner might issue a new smart card to the user and follow the registration phase.

2.13.5 Cryptanalysis of Wu-Xu-Xiang Scheme

The scheme presented above is traceable. Traceability attack can easily be launched against the scheme, therefore, suffered from security flaws.

2.14 Lipping Zhang et al.'s Scheme

Recently Zhang et al.'s presented another three-factor authentication scheme for chaotic map-based symmetric cryptography using smart card. The protocol contains five stages: the initialization, the registration, the login, the authentication and the change of password / biometrics phases, each described under the following headings:

Symbols	Description
S	Server
U_i	User
SC	Smart card
ID_i	Identity

PW_i	Password
B_i	Biometric template
mk	master server key
h(.)	hash algorithm
H(.)	Bio-Hashing Algorithm
E_k(.)	Private key k encryption
D_k(.)	Private key k decryption
Δ	Matching Algorithm
⊕	X-OR operation
‖	Concatenation operation

Table- 13: Notations used Lipping Zhang et al.'s Scheme

2.14.1 Initialization Phase

The remote server chooses a high entropy random digit for making the master secrete key mk, h(.) and a private key encipherment technique E_k(.) and decipherment technique D_k(.).

2.14.2 Registration Phase

All the computations in this phase take place between the user and server through a private route. This stage consists of the below steps:

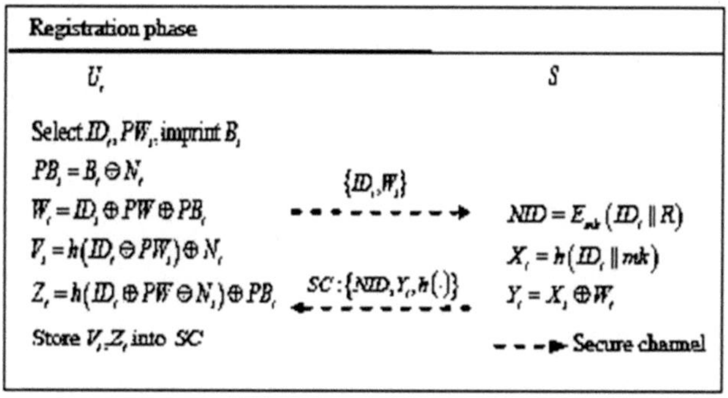

```
Registration phase
        U_i                                              S
Select ID_i, PW_i, imprint B_i
PB_i = B_i ⊖ N_i
W_i = ID_i ⊕ PW ⊕ PB_i         {ID_i, W_i}
V_i = h(ID_i ⊖ PW_i) ⊕ N_i    ─ ─ ─ ─ ─ ─ ─►    NID = E_mk(ID_i ‖ R)
Z_i = h(ID_i ⊕ PW ⊖ N_i) ⊕ PB_i   SC:{NID,Y_i,h(.)}    X_i = h(ID_i ‖ mk)
Store V_i,Z_i into SC          ◄ ─ ─ ─ ─ ─ ─     Y_i = X_i ⊕ W_i
                                                 ─ ─ ─► Secure channel
```

Figure- 22: The Registration

R1: U_i takes ID_i and PW_i, provide biometrics B_i through a sensor, then it generates a random number N_i and calculate $PB_i = B_i \oplus N_i$, $W_i = ID_i \oplus PW_i \oplus PB_i$, $V_i h(ID_i \oplus PW_i) \oplus N_i$ and $Z_i = h(ID_i \oplus PW_i \oplus N_i) \oplus PB_i$, relayes {$ID_i$, W_i} through a secure channel to the server.

R2: Upon getting $\{ID_i, PW_i\}$ message, the server checks the ID_i in the identity table and selects a number R to create dynamic identity $NID = E_{mk}(ID_i\|R)$ and calculates $X_i = h(ID_i\|mk)$, $Y_i = X_i \oplus W_i$ and send back $\{NID, Y_i, h(.)\}$ into the terminal for smart card.

R3: By receiving the message $\{NID, Y_i, h(.)\}$ the user stores $\{Z_i, V_i\}$ in the memory safely. The final value in the memory becomes $\{NID, Y_i, h(.), Z_i, V_i, x\}$ as show in the figure below:

2.14.3 Login Phase

In this phase the user performs below steps:

L1: Legitimate user provides smart card in the machine, chooses ID_i, PW_i and biometrics B_i^*.

L2: Smart card calculates $N_i = V_i \oplus h(ID_i \oplus PW_i)$, $PB_i = h(ID_i \oplus PW_i \oplus N_i) \oplus Z_i$ and $PB_i^* = B_i^* \oplus N_i$ and compare the biometric with the stored values by using Δ-algorithm, i.e. $\Delta(PB_i^*, PB_i)$, if successful then proceeded to the next step otherwise rejects and terminated automatically.

L3: Smart card also selects another digit say u, calculate $T_u(x)$, $W_i = ID_i \oplus PW_i \oplus PB_i$, $X_i = Y_i \oplus W_i$ and $a_i = h(ID_i\|X_i\|T_u(x))$ and relays $m_1 = \{NID, a_i, T_u(x)\}$ to the server through a private channel.

2.14.4 Authentication Phase

The server and terminal accomplish the below mention computations for obtaining a successful common authentication as shown in the figure:

A1: Decrypt the original NID using mk and checks it with the stored value in the identity table and computes $X'_i = h(ID'\|mk)$ and verify it with $a_i = h(ID'_i\| X'_i\| T_u(x))$, if not the process terminated, and if yes the random number say R^* and s are created for new dynamic identity $NID^* = E_{mk}(ID^*_i\|R^*)$ and calculates the shared session key $sk_S = h(T_S\|T'_u(x))$. The server computes $M = h(sk_S\|ID'_i) \oplus NID^*$ and $b_i = h(ID'_i\|sk_S\|NID^*\|NID)$ and relays $m_2 = \{b_i, M, T_S(x)\}$ to the legitimate user over an insecure channel.

A2: The smart card calculates $sk_u = h(T_u(T_S(x))$ for obtaining the dynamic identity $NID^* = M \oplus h(sk_u\|ID_i)$ and check the values of b_i is same at $h(ID_i\|sk_u\|NID^*\|NID)$, if so the smart card compute $c_i = h(ID_i\|sk_u\|NID^*)$ and provide $m_3 = \{c_i\}$ to the server over an insecure channel. And if the value of b_i is not equal in both the equations, then the server understands that this is an old message, which could be discarded and the processes finished.

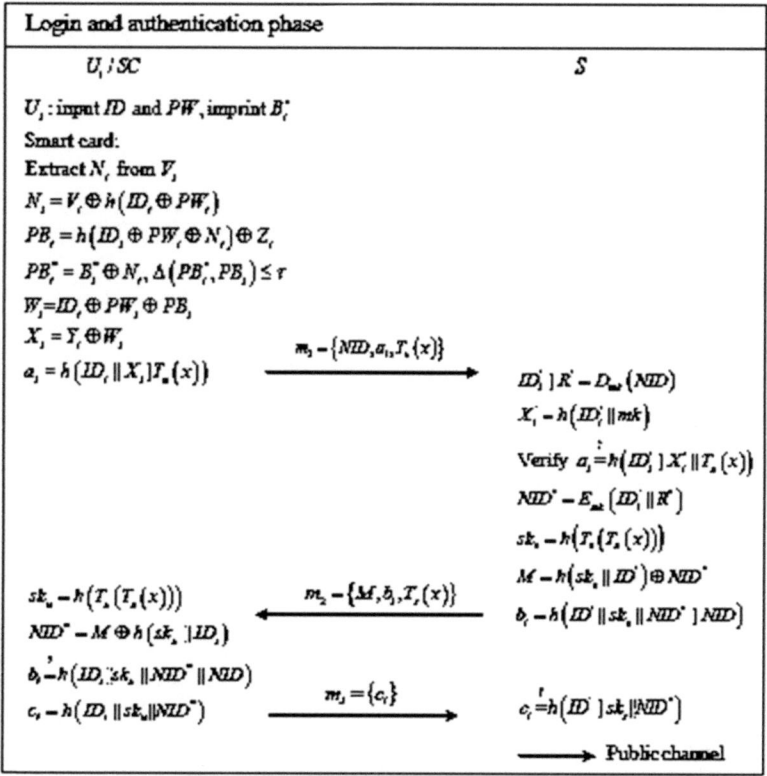

Figure- 23: Login and Authentication Phases

A3: By getting m_3, the server calculates $h(ID'_i\|sk_u\|NID^*)$ and verify for result in c_i, if a case not equal finished otherwise the server understand that the user is a legal one as shown below:

2.14.5 Password or Biometric Updating Phase

The legal user might provide the facility of changing / updating her or his smart card password / biometrics easily, freely and securely. This phase involves the following steps of calculations:

P1: Smart card owner need to inserts it in the terminal, provides ID_i, PW_i and B^*_i upon demand.

P2: The smart card calculates $N_i = V_i \oplus h(ID_i \oplus PW_i)$, $PB_i = h(ID_i \oplus PW_i \oplus N_i) \oplus Z_i$ and $PB_1^* = B_i^* \oplus N_i$, match both biometrics, if matching occurs {*request a new password and biometric*} message has been relayed, and if a matching is beyond the values, rejects the request.

P3: The user chooses a new password PB_i^{new}, an integer nine and new biometrics been using a sensor.

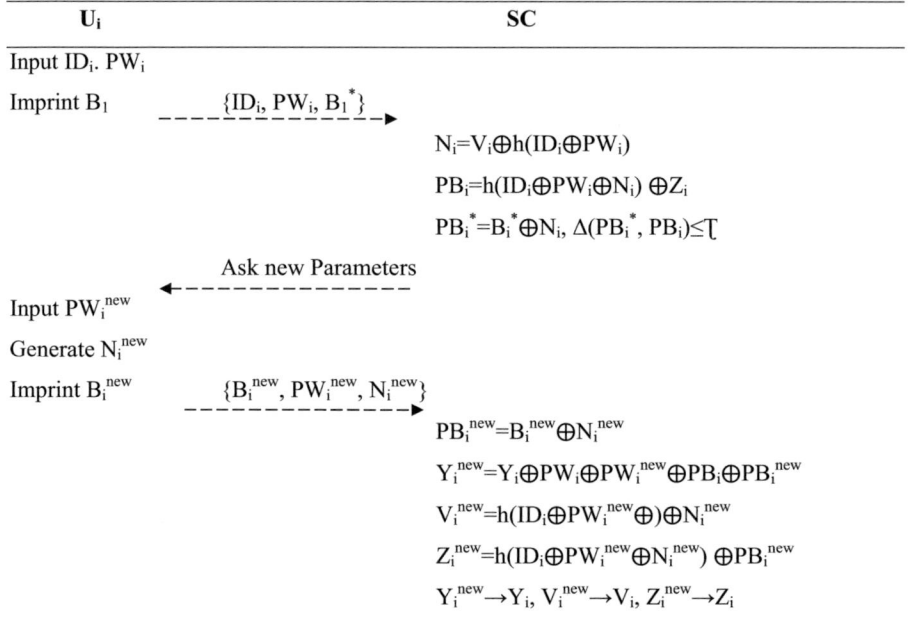

Password and Biometrics update phase

P4: By getting the values the smart card calculates $PB_i^{new} = B_i^{new} \oplus N_i^{new}$ $Y_i^{new} = T_i \oplus PW_i \oplus PW_i^{new} \oplus PB_i \oplus PB_i^{new}$, $V_i^{new} = h(ID_i \oplus PW_i^{new} \oplus N_i^{new}$ $Z_i^{new} = h(ID_i \oplus PW_i^{new} \oplus N_i^{new\,+}) \oplus PB_i^{new}$ and replaces the old values Y_i, V_i, Z_i} with { Y_i^{new}, V_i^{new}, Z_i^{new}} individually.

2.14.6 Cryptanalysis of Lipping Zhang et al.'s Scheme

This scheme not yet breaks by anyone. Different attacks have been launched, but much secure against all known attacks.

2.15 Zhang et al.'s Scheme

Developing a good verification significant arrangement scheme for Session Initiation Protocol is quite a tough job from the perspective of together performance and security, because performance and security of an exchange information as two serious issues affecting Session Initiation (SIP) submission continuously appear inconsistent. The scheme discussed below is biometric-based, lightweight and symmetric encryption using smart card is a powerful tool for authentication. The scheme might gain a slight stability among performance and safety. As described below:

	Notations Used
S_i	Server	U_i	User
ID_i	User	BT_i	Biometric Template
Δ	Matching function	sk	session key
$\parallel$	Concatenation function	m$\parallel$n	m concatenated with n
$\oplus$	X-OR function	%	modulus
$E_x(P)$	Message P encrypted with key X	PW_i	Password
$D_X(P)$	Message P decrypted by key X		

Table- 14: Notation Used for Zhang et al.'s Scheme

2.15.1 Registration Phase

For user's registration, calculation completed in two steps i.e.:

Reg1: U_L chooses ID_L, PW_L, create Biometric B_{io}. Choosing an integer digit named ∂, $X_1 = \partial \oplus B_{io}$. This value is combined with identity and password $Y_1 = PW_L \oplus X_1 \oplus \partial$. Now $Z_1 = h(PW_L \oplus ID_L) \oplus \partial$. The U_L then provides {ID_L, Y_1, $h(.)$} to server S_L over a private route.

Reg2: The S_L selects it's hidden key S for private key encryption/decryption. The process of $E_K(.)$ and $D_K(.)$ is completed on the server side as shown below:

User U	Server S
Chooses ID_L, PW_L, ∂, $h(.)$	
Produce biometric B_{io}	
Calculate $X_1 = \partial \oplus B_{io}$	
$\quad Y_1 = PW_L \oplus EB \oplus ID_L$	
$\quad Z_1 = h(PW_L \oplus ID_L) \oplus \partial \quad \xrightarrow{\{ID_L,\ Y_1,\ h(.)\}}$	
	Select server private key "K"
	for $E_K(.)$ & $D_K(.)$ i.e.

Chapter 2   Literature Review

$$\text{Computes } I = E_K(ID_L)$$
$$J_1 = E_K(ID \oplus K)$$
$$P_1 = J_1 \oplus Y_1$$
$$Q_1 = E_K(Y_1)$$

⟵ Smart card $\{(I, Q_1, P_1)\}$

Store $\{X_1, Z_1, h(.)\}$ into smart card

The Registration Phase

2.15.2 Login and Authentication Phases

These phases performed the following computations:

LA1: U_L provides smart card for logging into the system and inputs ID_L, PW_L creates Biometrics B_{io}. At this stage the smart card retrieves a big integer number say α from the equation Z_1 $h(PW_L \oplus ID_L)$. Now by means of α and B_{io}, $X_1^{'} = α \oplus B_{io}$ match the two values. If done calculation starts to otherwise reject.

At the moment smart card calculate $J_1^{'} = K \oplus PW_L \oplus X_1 \oplus ID_L$ by he stored values $\{P_1, X_1\}$, the server Verify the equation $E_J(PW_L \oplus X_1 \oplus ID_L) = L$ if satisfied the remote server chooses another number m and calculate $R_1 = ((PW_L \oplus X_1 \oplus ID_L) \| m)$ and $R_2 = E_J(P_1 \| ID_L \| R_1)$, after this he user puts a **REQUEST (I, R_2)** message to SIP server through un-secure route.

LA2: S_L decrypts the request message using K check ID_L in the stored identity in the database on the server, if a match occurs, then the ID_L chooses it's private key K to calculate $V_1 = E_K(ID_L \oplus K)$ and also decrypts the request message C_2 by the help of K. The S_L matches the values of ID_L using $P_1 = Q_1 \oplus V_1$ and decrypt V_1, $V_i^{'}$ and calculate whether both values holds $R_3 = PW_L \oplus X_1 \oplus ID_L \oplus b$ and $PW_L \oplus X_1 \oplus ID_L$ in C_1 if ok, server selects two random numbers m and b, secure hash and calculates $Z_1 = h(m \oplus b)$ and produce $Auth_s = E_K(C_3 \| C_4)$ from $C_3 = PW_L \oplus X_1 \oplus IDL \oplus b$ and $C_4 = (h(m \oplus R_3) \| m)$. At the end server puts challenge tone

Challenge (realm, Auths, S1) to UL.

User U	Server S
Provide ID_L, PW_L and integer digit m	
Scan iris to obtain B_{io}^{*}	
$X_1^{'} = m \oplus B_{io}^{*}$ and Match $\Delta(X_1, X_1^{'})$	
$V_1^{'} = Q_1 \oplus PW_L \oplus X_1 \oplus ID_L$	
Verify $E_K(PW_L \oplus X_1 \oplus ID_L) = W_1$	

$C_1 = ((PW_L \oplus X_1 \oplus ID_L) \| m)$

$C_2 = E_v(Q_1 \| ID_L \| C_1)$

REQUEST (I, C$_2$) →

Decrypt I to and check it in identity storage

$V_1 = E_K(ID \oplus K)$

$D_K(C_2)$ using V_1

Calculate the 2 IDs

$P_1 = Q_1 \oplus V_1$

Confirm $P_1 = PW_L \oplus X_1 \oplus ID_L$

chooses S_1, b

$Z_1 = h(m \oplus b)$

$C_3 = PW_L \oplus X_1 \oplus ID_L \oplus b$

$C_4 = (h(m \oplus C_3) \| m)$

$Auth_s = E_K(C_3 \| C_4)$

← CHALLENGE (realm, Auth$_s$, S$_1$)

$D_K(Auth_s)$ using V_1'

$C_3 \oplus PW_L \oplus X_1 \oplus ID_L$ to get b

Confirm $C_4 = (h(m \oplus C_3) \| m)$ and sets $Z_1' = h(m \oplus b)$

$Auth_U = h(m \oplus b \| (S_1 + 1))$

RESPONSE (realm, Auth$_u$) →   Auth$_u$=h(m⊕b∥(S$_1$+1))

Login and Authentication Phases

LA3: Upon obtaining challenge tone from the server side the U_L decrypts $Auth_s$ getting C_3 and C_4. Smart card draw b from C_3, PW_L, ID_L and X_1 and calculates $(h(m \oplus C_3 \| m))$ and confirm these beliefs, if seen ok calculation proceeded obtaining $Z_1 = h(m \oplus b)$ also confirmation message $Auth_U = h(m \oplus b \| (S_1+1))$. Then the U_L relays **RESPONSE (realm, Auth$_u$) message** to the SIP server.

LA4: SIP server authenticates whether the quantities hold $Auth_U = h(m \oplus b \| (S_1+1))$. If so, SIP server sets $Z_1' = h(a \oplus b)$ as shared key; otherwise, commutation stop and the processes become ends.

2.15.3 Password Change Phase

The legitimate U_L can easily change their password without facing any hurdles. The following steps of computations are performed:

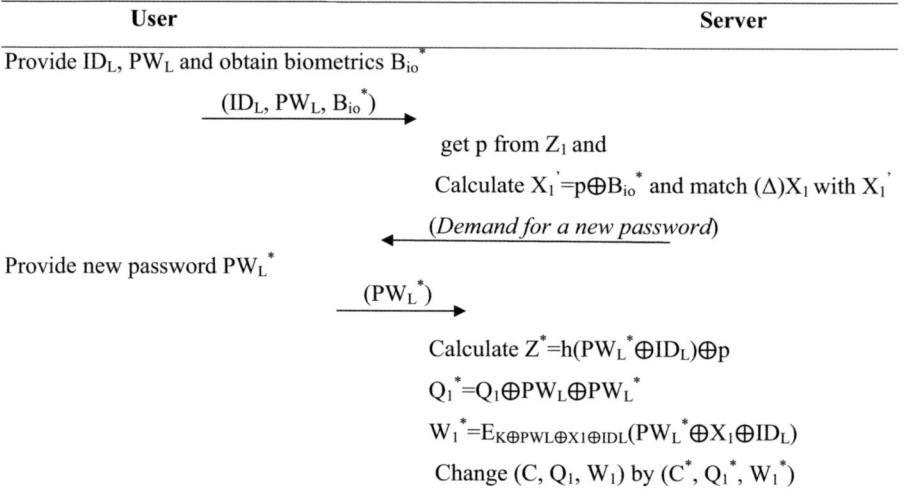

Password Change Phase

Step (i): Smart card calculates h $(PW_L \oplus ID_L)$ by mean of PW_L, ID_L and draw a extraordinary arbitrary digit p from $Z_1 \oplus h(PW_L \oplus ID_L)$ and calculates $X_1' = p \oplus B_{io}*$ from p and getting biometric $B_{io}{}^*$ and verify Δ (X_1', X_1) if so, demanding for a new password from the user.

Step (ii): U_L provides fresh password $PW_L{}^*$ and relays it into the smart card.

Step (iii): The smart card calculates and changed it according to the demand put by the user.

2.16 Zhang et al.'s Protocol Analysis

The Zhang et al.'s [15] protocol is a three-factor authentication scheme based on symmetric cryptography has a well-verbalized, despite, the scheme has many drawbacks. Because the protocol has the potential for more suitable improvements that can be added towards the safety and computational cost optimizations. We have effort to solve the drawbacks and security issues in the scheme by presenting an enhanced authentication scheme.

2.16.1 Working Procedure of the Scheme

The Zhang et al.'s protocol working procedures are defined under the following four steps:

- ➤ The legitimate user directs a REGUEST to the remote server

- The remote server submits CHALLENGE (nonce, realm) to the legitimate user, where nonce is created by the remote server while realm is the message digest.
- The legitimate user computes the CHALLENGE (nonce, realm) message and produced a RESPONSE h (nonce, realm, Identity, values) and communicates to the remote server.

- The remote server cuts the password as described in the Identity and confirm it where it is according to the pre-defined one. If match the remote server computes the one-way hash value and check it with the previously received RESPONSE value. If found equal the legitimate user verified and communication starts.

The drawbacks of the scheme [15] are as under:

2.16.2 Biometric Extraction and Password Guessing Attacks

The attacker recovers EB and SR from smart card recovers biometric from the stolen smart card by using the following steps.

1. First, Attacker computes X=EB $\oplus$ SR, where X = B$\oplus$ h(PW$\oplus$ID)
2. Assuming, the users ID is also hacked by the attacker. Then, it calculates the password by trying various combinations of PW* and checking the equality match for the following.
3. r*=H(PW* $\oplus$ ID) $\oplus$ SR
4. B*=H(PW* $\oplus$ ID) $\oplus$ X
5. EB ?=r*$\oplus$ B*

2.16.3 User Anonymity Violation

User anonymity is an extremely compulsory feature of user authentication schemes. In this extensive computing period, person's sensitive private evidence, such as favorites, existences, community engagements and habitations etc., are likely to need an attacker for various purposes, e.g., by examining session evidence in a necessary task performing time, services or assets existing and access of exact time interval during transaction. Therefore, recently the privacy of anyone is fast growing amongst individuals, governments and organizations, confidentiality-protecting cryptographic functions are of special attention. Furthermore, in cell phone situations, an attacker can also achieve or expose owner is personal information for tracing the object's present site and movement's details. Hence, User Anonymity predominantly well-regarded property of far-flung authentication schemes and is a vital goal for anyone. This feature cannot preserve in Zhang's et al.'s scheme [15].

2.16.4 Replay Attack and Denial-of-Service Attack

Initially, after the legitimate user directs a REQUEST (I, C_2) message to the remote server, an adversary can copy it and launch a replay attack on the server any other time. At this stage the server computes $E_s(ID \oplus s)$ and $R = T \oplus V$ and can easily verify $R ?= PW \oplus EB \oplus ID$. In this manner the server will be forced to generate the CHALLENGE message. The remote server will investigate the legitimacy of an adversary in the incoming stage of a RESPONSE message created by an attacker. A Denial-of-Service (DoS) attack could be launched beside the server by an adversary in this regards. The attacker might disturb the capable working of the remote server by initiating a Denial-of-Service attack.

2.17 Chapter Summary

A major difficulty in the information security is the authenticity of the message over the communication line between two parties to start a secure data exchange. Several different techniques were proposed by different researchers like password-based authentication protocols, and two factors authentication protocols. But these protocols showed many security weaknesses, including guessing of password (Online/Offline), replay, masquerade, impersonation, insider, server spoofing and many other attacks. To overcome these security vulnerabilities a biometric-based authentication protocols were designed. Because biometric keys are difficult to steal, share, allocate and distribute. Biometric based authentication scheme is tremendously hard to guesstimate easily and somebody's biometrics cannot easily break down.

In this chapter the necessary schemes of different researcher have been studied and put their importance. Also at the end of every scheme, weaknesses also discuss. Different attacks launched on these scheme, because to highlight the information security and cryptographic functions importance.

Chapter 3: Proposed Solution

3.1 Overview

Maximum security protocols are particularly very simple if only their size is measured. But, the properties they are made-up to guarantee for secure information exchange, are tremendously difficult, and therefore, it is hard to develop protocols exact just by unconstrained thoughts and tell. Designing a riskless protocol is much difficult task. We have proposed a robust, lightweight, three-factor authentication scheme from a number of features for designing it. The proposed scheme are described formally and informally after our complete analysis of existing authentication schemes, we have establish some remaining problems, specifically, certain are excessively common and practical; several are ambiguous so that designers are rigid to possession; some express only thought, not to read how to figure protocols and avoid faults. We put forward methods against replay attacks, Denial-of-Service attacks and how to make a scheme anonymous to become untraceable, by examining the attack appearances and the causes for attack. A huge number of illustrations show that the proposed protocol is simple, effective and practical. Also maximum existing authentication schemes are based on heavyweight cryptographic primitives i.e. ECC, RSA or Diffie-Hellman Key Exchange Techniques etc. and the schemes based on lightweight symmetric key primitives have drawbacks like user anonymity violation, have suffered from replay attack for which later on DoS attack also launched and many more.

3.2 Proposed Scheme

This research is mainly focuses on the drawbacks of the already existing authentication schemes based on symmetric key primitives and information security flaws of scheme [15].

So for the enhanced proposed scheme consists of biometric characteristics. The smart card has the talent of checking the originality of the biometric data because a pre-defined template will be stored before purchase a smart card. Even if the smart card was theft no one can extract the biometric characteristics due to using BioHashing technique. The following computations occur for user biometric characteristics.

$HB = H(BT_{ia})$ and $HB' = H(BT_{ia}^*)$ and match $\Delta(HB, HB')$ or $\Delta (BT_{ia}, BT_{ia}^*) = \Delta (F_k(BT_{ia}), F_k(BT_{ia}^*))$: Where BT_{ia} represent Biometric Template and BT_{ia}^* represents extracted biometrics, F_k is a function with secrete key k. After satisfaction of the above mentioned equations, the smart card has the ability to perform function. We use XOR bitwise operation

⊕ and random integer number of high entropy q is a private key. The matching of biometric is shown in figure-1 and figure-2

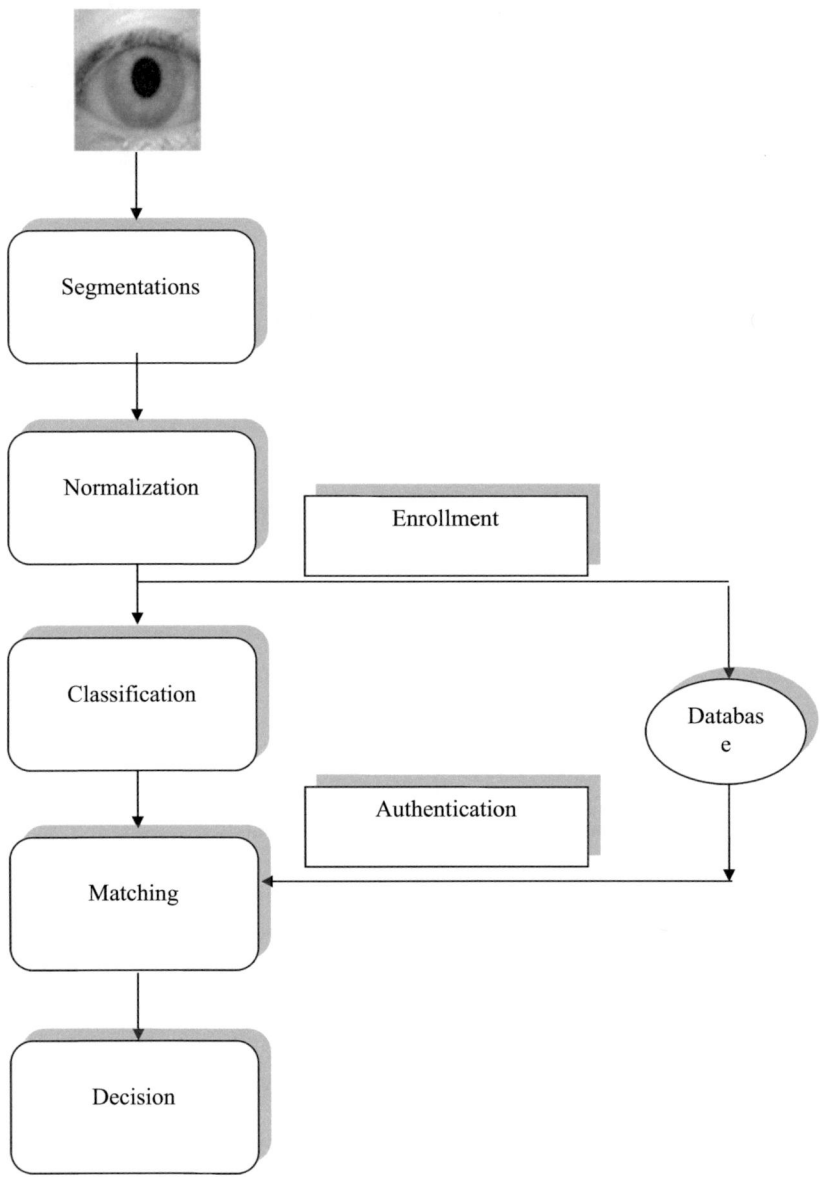

Figure- 24: Iris BioHashing Technique

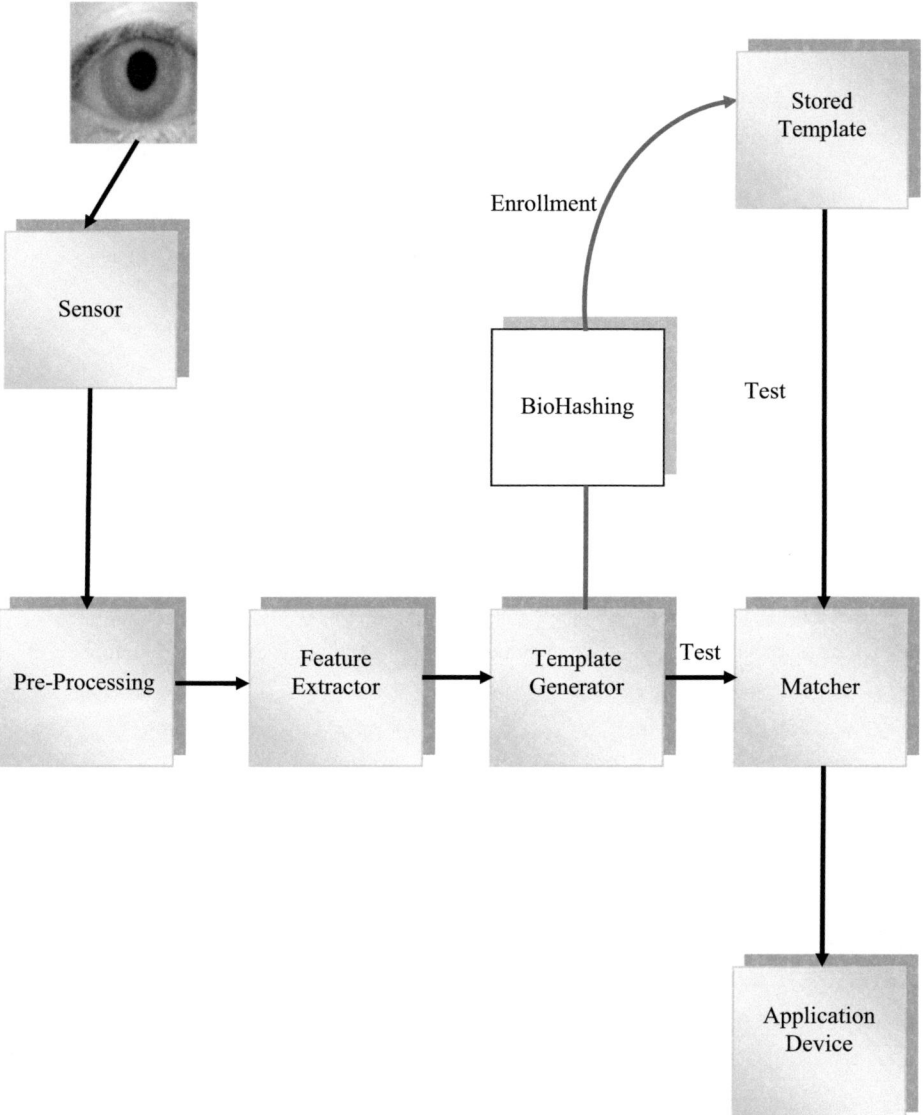

Figure- 25: Biometric Template Storing Stages

The proposed scheme is mainly consists of three entities i.e. password, biometrics and smart card, and is divided into three phases: registration, login and authentication and password change phases. Each of which is briefly described under the following headings.

Symbols and its Description			
U_{ia}	User's A	S_{ia}	Server's A
ID_{ia}	User's A Identity	PW_{ia}	User's A Password
BT_{ia}	User's A Biometrics	BT_{ia}^{*}	User's A input Biometric
Δ	Matching Algorithm	$h(.)$	Secure Hash Algorithm
S	Private key of S_{ia}	HB	BioHashing
sk	Shared Session Key	$\|\|$	Concatenation function
$\oplus$	X-OR symbol	T	Timestamp

Table- 15: Notation used for the Proposed Scheme

3.2.1 Registration Phase

Whenever a legitimate user U_{ia} desires to roll with the remote server S_{ia}, it executes the succeeding procedure with the remote server in the registration phase.

R1: $U_{ia} \Rightarrow S_{ia}$:(HB, ID_{ia}, N)

The user U_{ia} selects his/her individuality ID_{ia}, password PW_{ia} and ensures an iris scan as biometrics to generate biometric template BT_{ia}. The BioHashing technique HB is applied to keep it secret HB=H (BT_{ia}), Then chooses an integer number of high entropy q and one-way hash function h (.) :{ zero, one}$^{*} \rightarrow$ {zero, one}^{k} M = HB$\oplus$q, N = $PW_{ia} \oplus ID_{ia} \oplus$M and O = h (M $\oplus PW_{ia} \oplus ID_{ia}) \oplus$q and transmit { HB, N, ID_{ia}} over a secure channel ($\Rightarrow$).

R2: $S_{ia} \rightarrow U_{ia}$:(A, F)

The remote server chooses a secrete key "S" and encrypt the ID_{ia} along with the current time stamp t_{so} i.e. A = $E_S(ID_i \| t_{so})$. Also encrypt ID_{ia} along with bitwise XOR of the server secrete key S i.e. B = $E_S(ID_i \oplus S)$, using N to encrypt B i.e. F = $E_j(B)$ and submit {A, F} to the memory of smart card for future usage.

R3: The already stored values in the smart card {O, N} only N become hashing here P =h(N), while receiving {A, F} finally the memory of smart card have {O, P, A, F}

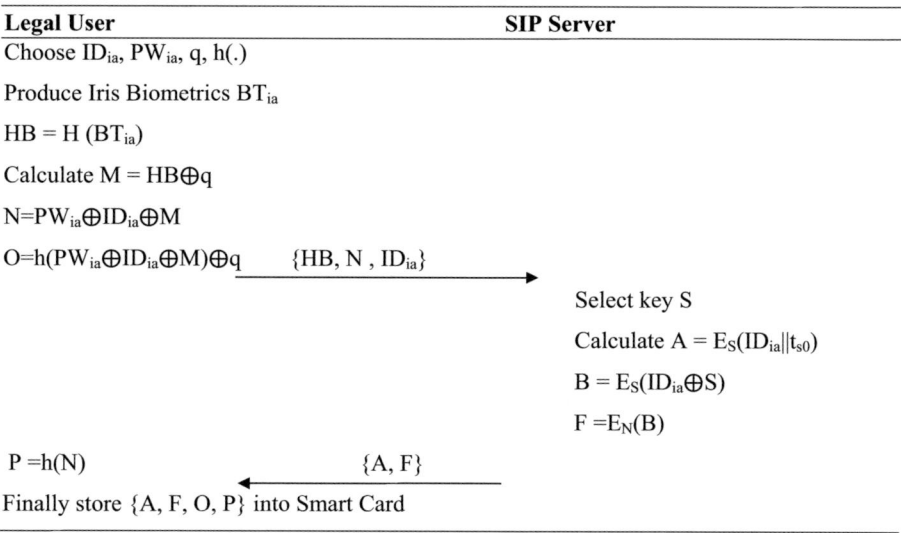

The Registration Phase

3.2.2 Login and Authentication Phases

LA1: Legitimate user's A (U_{ia}) inserts his/her smart card into the machine capable for it and input ID_{ia}, PW_{ia} and Iris shot to produce Biometrics BT_{ia}^*. BioHashing technique is applied to secure the biometrics $HB' = H(BT_{ia})$. Then smart card regains random number of high entropy q from the already stored values in the memory of smart card $q = O \oplus h(PW_{ia} \oplus ID_{ia} \oplus HB')$. The U_{ia} computes $N' = PW_{ia} \oplus ID_{ia} \oplus HB' \oplus$ by means of the already stored information in the memory of smart-card to confirm the calculation $P \stackrel{?}{=} h(N')$ if become ok on both entities (smart card and biometric) then decrypt F using N' i.e. $B = D_{N'}(F)$. Next chooses freshness/timestamp T_1, calculate $R_1 = h(B\|ID_{ia}\|T_1)$ and $R_2 = E_B(P\|ID_{ia}\|R1\|T1)$. Finally submit a REQUEST (A, R_1, R_2, T_1) towards the server through insecure public channel ($\rightarrow$).

LA2: The server deducts the initial timestamp from the current one and compares it with the predefined threshold timestamp of the server, also decrypt the user's identity from the received values using a secret key s and verifying ID_{ia} in its identity table, if doesn't exist the processing terminated otherwise calculate $B = E_s(ID_{ia} \oplus S)$. Check $R_1 \stackrel{?}{=} h(B\|ID_{ia}\|T_1)$, if found equal then decrypt the value of R_2 using B and selects n put a shared session key $sk = h(p \oplus n)$ and compute $R_3 = E_B(n\|sk\|T_{s1})$ and $A_n = E_s(ID_{ia}\|T_{s1})$, where A_n is the combination of ID_{ia} with the second time stamp values of the server. At the end the SIP server place a CHALLENGE (R_3, A_n, T_{s1}) to the legitimate user U_{ia}.

LA3: After receiving the challenge message, U_{ia} check the timestamp with the server time value (T_2') and match with the threshold time by the user, for the purpose of knowing that whether the value is received from the valid server or not. If it does not match, the computation session terminated. Otherwise the user U_{ia} decrypts R_3 using B. Also put a session key $sk' = h(p \oplus n)$ and check $sk'\ ?= sk$, if found true, the user keep sk is a shared session key. Now subtract time from the user identity A_n for the reason of later usage.

User	Server
Introduce smart card and enter ID_{ia} and PW_{ia}, and choose p	
Iris scan to obtain BT_{ia}^*	
Extract q from $O \oplus h(PW_{ia} \oplus ID_{ia} \oplus HB')$	
Calculate $HB' = H(BT_{ia}^*)$	
Compute $N' = PW_{ia} \oplus ID_{ia} \oplus HB' \oplus q$	
Check $P\ ?= h(N')$	
$B = D_{N'}(F)$	
Calculate $R_1 = h(B\|ID_{ia}\|T_1)$ and	
$R_2 = E_B(P\|ID_{ia}\|R_1\|T_1)$	
$\xrightarrow{\text{REQUEST }\{A, R_1, R_2, T_1\}}$	
	Comparing $(T_1' - T_1)$ against ΔT
	Decrypt A for ID_{ia} and check in the Identity table
	$ID_{ia}\|t_{s0} = D_S(A)$
	Calculate $B = E_s(ID_{ia} \oplus S)$
	Check $R_1\ ?= h(B\|ID_{ia}\|T_1)$
	Decrypt R_2 by using B and select n
	$(P\|ID_{ia}\|R_1\|T_1) = D_B(R_2)$
	Calculate $sk = h(p \oplus n)$
	$R_3 = E_B(n\|sk\|T_{s1})$
	$A_n = E_s(ID_{ia}\|T_{s1})$
$\xleftarrow{\text{CHALLENGE }\{R_3, A_n, T_{s1}\}}$	
Comparing $(T_2' - T_{s1})$ against ΔT	
Decrypt R_3 by using B i.e. $n\|sk' = D_B(R_3)$ and compute	
$sk' = h(p \oplus n)$	
Check $sk'\ ?= sk$ if true keep sk as shared secrete key	

The Login and Authentication Phases

Chapter 3 — Proposed Solution

3.2.3 Password Change Phase

In this phase of the proposed scheme the legitimate user U_{ia} can change his/her password easily and steadily. Also the user U_{ia} doesn't need to interact with the server, all the processes are completed between terminal and smart card. The following steps are performed during password change phase:

PC1: First-of-all the legitimate user inserts his/her smart card into the machine and makes an iris scan to generate a biometric template BT_{ia}^{*}, provide ID_{ia} and password PW_{ia} and relays a message $\{ID_{ia}, PW_{ia}, BT_{ia}^{*}\}$ to smart card as show below:

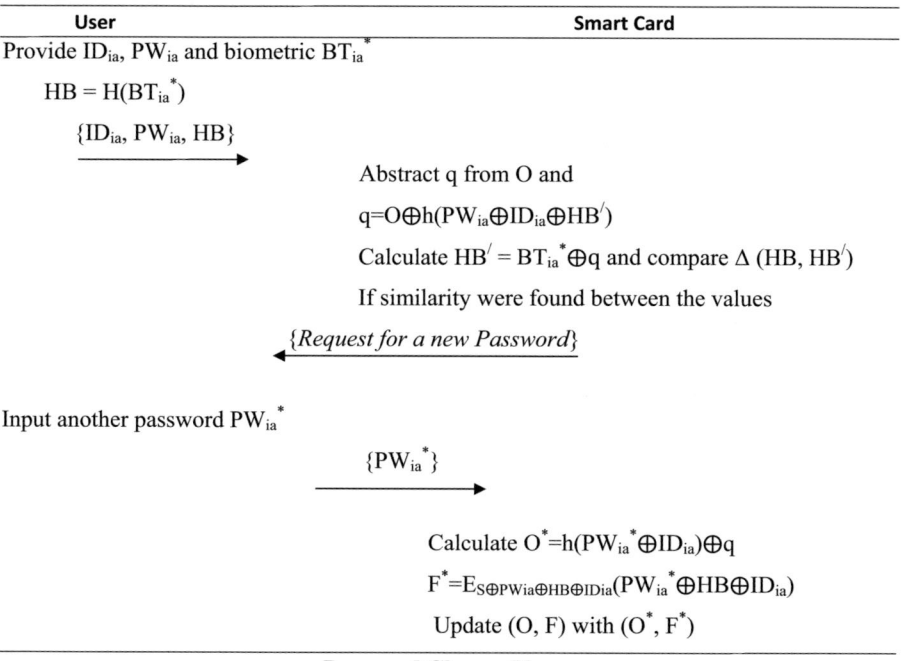

Password Change Phase

PC2: Generate random number "q" from the stored values of smart card, that is $q = O \oplus h(PW_{ia} \oplus ID_{ia} \oplus HB')$ and calculates $HB' = BT_{ia}^{*} \oplus q$ and associates it with the stored template BT_{ia}, that is $HB = BT_{ia} \oplus q$. If both found tally $\Delta(HB, HB')$ the smart card relays a message {demand for new password} to the user and if the values is behind the pretended value the process terminated.

PC3: After getting {request a new password} message from smart card, he/she inputs the new values PW_{ia}^{*} and directs to the smart card.

PC4: The smart card calculates $O^*=h(ID_{ia}\oplus PW_{ia}^*)\oplus q$ and $F^*=E_{HB\oplus IDia\oplus PWia}(HB\oplus ID_{ia}\oplus PW_{ia}^*)$ separately and the value at the smart card $\{O, F\}$ with $\{O^*, F^*\}$.

3.3 Chapter Summary

Security protocol is an analytical factor of the framework compulsory for protected communication and treating information. Before scheming and examining protocols, it is significant to moderate unnecessary work. In this chapter, we conferred the procedures to avoid replay attacks, DoS attacks and make the user untraceable (anonymous) on the protocols. We have already studied and mentioned the two types of attacks and user anonymity violation of the protocol. Then we conferred some ethics for securing the protocols. We also offered some approaches for designing the security protocols and then we tried to improve the protocol with the procedures offered. A number of examples in the literature have also been shown that the work done in the document is very significant.

Chapter 4: Security Analysis

4.1 Overview

In this chapter, we analyze the security of our improved enhanced authentication scheme by considering the adversarial model defined in chapter 1. In the below subsections, we demonstrate that the proposed scheme is strong against all known attacks. At the end a Table shall be designed which illustrates the security features accessible by proposed protocol and an assessment of security features with interrelated existing protocols.

Since, thoughtful ideas of cryptographic protocols needed so that we can observe the information regarding protocol contestants and adversaries. Upon receiving a message by the contestants:

- Does he/she know who sent it?
- Does he/she know that the message is fresh?
- Does he/she know that it is never just a repetition of something from the past message?
- Does network investigator know who is talking to whom?

The above questions can be covered here in this chapter i.e. deceivability, unassailability and extensiveness might be cater using BAN-logic with veneration to secure information exchange systems. The security analysis of the proposed scheme can be divided into two parts: Formal Security Analysis and Informal Security Analysis:

4.2 Formal Security Analysis

In web technology the communication participants not only share information and correspondence each other but they also use some defining rules called protocol that how to communicate. These protocols have turned to be more essential in web technology for the question how to secure the exchanged information from the attacker. In any rules designing, cryptographic functions are also needed for some specific problems solution inside a protocol In part-I the formal security analysis of the proposed scheme have been demonstrated by using BAN [16, 28] logic and an automated software toolkit called ProVerif [29-30]. BAN method used to prove that the proposed scheme achieves common authentication, can resist all known attacks and accomplish preferred characteristics.

4.2.1 BAN Logic

A formal-method for expressing and investigating an authentication protocols was first recommended in late 1980's. Since expansion in the area of cryptography and network security which has been encouraged on covering and altering the acceptance of the essential BAN logic.

"BAN is derived from the names of its authors, Burrows, Abadi and Needham. It is the first in a family of eponymous authentication logics. BAN is a logic of belief. The intended use of BAN is to analyze authentication protocols by deriving the beliefs that honest principles correctly executing a protocol can come to as a result of the protocol execution. BAN has been highly successful in uncovering protocol flaws, needed ASSUMPTIONS, etc., and it is relatively easy to use".

Terminologies and its Description	
"$P \mid \equiv Q$"	"P believes Q"
"# (X)"	"X is fresh"
"$P \mid \sim Q$"	"P once said Q"
"$P \xleftrightarrow{K} Q$"	"P and Q both use key K"
"$P \triangleleft Q$"	"P sees Q"
"$\xrightarrow{K} P$"	"P has a public key K"
"$P \Rightarrow Q$"	"P has jurisdiction over Q"
$P \xLeftrightarrow{K} Q$	"P and Q shared private key K"
"$\{P\}_K$"	"P encrypted under key K"

Table- 16: Notations used by Burrows, Abadi and Needham

4.2.2 Rules of BAN Logic

Various rules were defined by **Burrows, Abadi and Needham** (scientist). The aims as to authenticate protocols, if any of rule violate by any protocol steps; then it should be considered a wrong one. These rules are as given below:

Rule 1: Message Meaning

$$\frac{P \ belives \ P \overset{K}{\leftrightarrow} Q \ received\{X\}_K}{P \ belives \ Q \ said \ X}$$

"It means that if P receives X encrypted with K and if P believes K is a good key for talking with Q, then P believes Q once said X".

Rule 2: Nonce Verification

$$\frac{P \ belives \ frsh(X) \quad P \ belives \ Q \ said \ X}{P \ belives \ Q \ belives \ X}$$

These rules permits advancement from prevous to current, X cannot consists any $E_K(.)$ writing. It sorts a common intelligence for proclamations, but what if X is a nonce N_i? It give the native sense of trust to say that one party belives a nonce N_i.

Rule 3: Jurisdiction

$$\frac{P \ belives \ Q \ control \ X \quad P \ belives \ Q \ belives \ X}{P \ belives \ X}$$

Foremost trusts regarding upright key, even nevertheless it is arbitrary series that at no time perceived before means "strength of control statement". If P tackle stickX means P cannot create an inaccuracy in declaring X.

Rule 4: Acceptance Conjuncatenation

$$\frac{P \ belives \ X \quad P \ belives \ Y}{P \ belives \ (X,Y)}$$

$$\frac{P \ belives \ Q \ belives \ (X,Y)}{P \ belives \ Q \ belives \ X}$$

$$\frac{P \ belives \ Q \ said \ (X,Y)}{P \ belives \ Q \ said \ X}$$

Concatenations of communication are not eminent from aggregations.

Rule 5: Freshness Conjuncatenation

$$\frac{P \ belives \ fresh \ (X)}{P \ belives \ fresh \ (X,Y)}$$

It means X is garden-fresh then the tone locating from X is also fresh because X in it. If we say P trusts X is fresh and fresh Y too, we can also say that P believes that X and Y both are fresh.

Rule 6: Seeing is receiving

$$\frac{P \text{ belives } P \overset{K}{\leftrightarrow} Q \quad P \text{ received } \{X\}_K}{P \text{ received } X}$$

$$\frac{P \text{ received } (X,Y)}{P \text{ received } X}$$

4.2.3 BAN Method for Protocol Analysis

To analyze a set of rules by BAN logic, four steps to be taken into consideration. Firstly, idealized (Overemphasize) the authentication scheme. Secondly, compose rules (assumptions) about the preliminary phase. Next, interpret the protocol and at the end practice the logic to originate the principles detained by the protocol, i.e.

1. Convert and derived the scheme to an idealized form.
2. Write an assumptions starting from initial state.
3. Logical formulations are close to the announcements of the scheme.

Logical guesses are practical to the suppositions and the declarations so that to determinethe views believed by the participants in the scheme.

4.2.4 BAN-Logic Postulates

The guessing or postulation of a range for specific reason is the number of self-regulating state of affairs necessary to strength fundamentals of the personal to consist the selection.

Postulate 1: For Common Key

$$\frac{P \mid \equiv Q \overset{K}{\leftrightarrow} P, \quad P \triangleleft \{X\}_K}{P \mid \equiv Q \mid \sim X}$$

i.e. if P trusts K common with Q and understands message X converted under the control of K, at that moment P trusts Q once said X. In this, we need assurance that P does not direct X; it should be sufficient on the way to evoke $\{X\}_K$.

Postulate 2: For Open Key

$$\frac{P \mid \equiv \overset{K}{\rightarrow} Q, \quad P \triangleleft \{X\}_{X^{-1}}}{P \mid \equiv Q \mid \sim X}$$

Chapter 4   Security Analysis

i.e. if P trusts that Y is common by means of Q and gets$\{X\}_{X^{-1}}$, then P trusts that Q onetime said X. This guessing completed for the reason the guidelines◁ given above; assurance$\{X\}_{X^{-1}}$ wasn't disinterested pronounce via P.

Postulate 3: For Private Key

$$\frac{P\mid\equiv Q\overset{Y}{\rightleftharpoons}P \;\triangleleft<X>_Y}{P\mid\equiv Q \quad\mid\sim X}$$

Postulate 4: For Nonce-Verification

$$\frac{P\mid\equiv\#(X),\quad P\mid\equiv Q\mid\sim X}{P\mid\equiv Q\mid\equiv X}$$

i.e. if P accepts as true X and might have expressed just recently, Q formerly believed X and P considers Q trusts X, then X essentially be pure text i.e. it hasn't take account of any sub plan of form $\{Y\}_K$.

Postulate 5: For Jurisdiction

$$\frac{P\mid\equiv Q \mapsto X,\quad P\mid\equiv Q\mid\equiv X}{P\mid\equiv X}$$

i.e. if P have confidence over Q and under jurisdiction in excess of X before P confidences Q on the reality of X.

Postulate 6: For belief operator

$$\frac{P\mid\equiv X, P\mid\equiv Y}{P\mid\equiv(X,Y)}, \qquad \frac{P\mid\equiv(X,Y)}{P\mid\equiv X} \quad \text{and} \quad \frac{P\mid\equiv Q\mid\equiv(X,Y)}{P\mid\equiv Q\mid\equiv X}$$

Postulate 7: For Similar Rule

$$\frac{P\mid\equiv Q\mid\sim(X,Y)}{P\mid\equiv Q\mid\sim X}$$

Postulate 8: For Basic Understands

$$\frac{P\triangleleft(X,Y)}{P\triangleleft x}$$

$$\frac{P\triangleleft<X>_Y}{P\triangleleft X}$$

73

$$\frac{P\mid\equiv Q\stackrel{K}{\leftrightarrow}P,\quad P\triangleleft\{X\}_K}{P\triangleleft X}$$

$$\frac{P\mid\equiv Q\stackrel{K}{\rightarrow}P,\quad P\triangleleft\{X\}_K}{P\triangleleft X}$$

$$\frac{P\mid\equiv Q\stackrel{K}{\rightarrow}P,\quad P\triangleleft\{X\}_{K^{-1}}}{P\triangleleft X}$$

Postulate 9: For Freshness

$$\frac{P\mid\equiv\#(X)}{P\mid\equiv\#(X,Y)}$$

Postulate 10: For Common Public key

$$\frac{P\mid\equiv R\stackrel{K}{\leftrightarrow}R'}{P\mid\equiv R'\stackrel{K}{\leftrightarrow}R}$$

$$\frac{P\mid\equiv Q\mid\equiv R\stackrel{K}{\leftrightarrow}R'}{P\mid\equiv Q\mid\equiv R'\stackrel{K}{\leftrightarrow}R}$$

Postulate 11: For the same Private Key

$$\frac{P\mid\equiv R\stackrel{X}{\rightleftharpoons}R'}{P\mid\equiv R'\stackrel{X}{\rightleftharpoons}R}$$

$$\frac{P\mid\equiv Q\mid\equiv R\stackrel{X}{\rightleftharpoons}R'}{P\mid\equiv Q\mid\equiv R'\stackrel{X}{\rightleftharpoons}R}$$

Postulate 12:

We can build confirmations logically by a method let say X and another method let say Y, if it is an order of $Z_0...Z_1......Z_n$ where $Y = Z_o$, $X = Z_n$, and every Z_{i+1} might achieved on or after preceding one following set of rules.

a) Let server S create uninformed common key between X and Y.

$$X\mid\equiv S\mapsto X\stackrel{K}{\leftrightarrow}Y$$

b) For unambiguous this quantification is…..

$$X \mid \equiv \forall K \ (S \mapsto X Y)$$

c) To sidestep uncertainties

$$X \mid \equiv \forall K \ (S \mapsto Y X \stackrel{K}{\leftrightarrow} Y)$$

$$X \mid \equiv S \mapsto \forall K \ (Y \mapsto X \stackrel{K}{\leftrightarrow} Y$$

4.2.5 BAN Idealized Form

We can convert every rule's steps into an idealized form.

Protocol Step	Description
$P \rightarrow Q: message$	P sends *message* to Q
$A \rightarrow B: \{A, K_{ab}\}_{K_{bs}}$	B know K_{bs} and K_{ab} another key to transfer with A.
$A \rightarrow B: \{A \stackrel{K_{ab}}{\leftrightarrow} B\}_{K_{bs}}$	Tells B, recognizes key K_{bs} and K_{ab} is another key to transfer with A.
$B \triangleleft \{A \stackrel{K_{ab}}{\leftrightarrow} B\}_{K_{bs}}$	B *sees* the communication of A and b via K_{ab} and K_{bs} is another key to transfer with A
$A \mid \equiv A \stackrel{K}{\leftrightarrow} B, \quad B \mid \equiv A \stackrel{K}{\leftrightarrow} B$	Confirmation is ok among A and B using K
$A \mid \equiv B \mid \equiv A \stackrel{K}{\leftrightarrow} B, B \mid \equiv A \mid \equiv A \stackrel{K}{\leftrightarrow} B$	A believes B believes that A transfer data to B using K and vice versa.
$A \mid \equiv \stackrel{K}{\rightarrow} B$	A believes communication to B over a public key K
$A \mid \equiv A \stackrel{N_a}{\rightleftharpoons} B$	A and B might share some private secretes

Table- 17: Protocol steps and its descriptions [28]

4.3 Proposed Protocol Analysis

Our scheme can be shown using BAN logic is summarized as follows:

Chapter 4 — Security Analysis

4.3.1 BAN Goals for the Proposed Scheme

Goal1: user $\models$ Server $\xleftrightarrow{sk}$ user

Goal2: Server $\models$ user $\models$ Server $\xleftrightarrow{sk}$ user

Goal3: user $\models$ Server $\xleftrightarrow{sk}$ user

Goal4: user $\models$ Server $\models$ Server $\xleftrightarrow{sk}$ user

4.3.2 BAN Idealized form for the Proposed Scheme

Idealization is used in BAN logic to show the central information regarding beliefs of the receiving parties in each step of the protocol. For the proposed procedure idealized form are as follow:

Message 1: user$\rightarrow$ Server: A, R_1, R_2, T_1: $\{A, ID_{ia}, R_1, R2, T_1\}_B$

Message 2: Server$\rightarrow$ user: R_3, A_n, T_{s1}: $\{R_3, A_n \parallel T_{s1}\}_B$

4.3.3 BAN Assumptions for the Proposed Scheme

Assumption 1: User $\models$ # (T_1)

Assumption 2: Server $\models$ # (p, n, T_{s1})

Assumption 3: User $\models$ Server $\xleftrightarrow{B}$ User

Assumption 4: Server $\models$ Server $\xleftrightarrow{B}$ User

Assumption 5: User $\models$ Server $\xleftrightarrow{sk = h(p\oplus n)}$ User

Assumption 6: Server $\models$ Server $\xleftrightarrow{sk = h(p\oplus n)}$ User

Assumption 7: User $\models$ Server $\Rightarrow$ (R_4, p)

Assumption 8: Server $\models$ User $\Rightarrow$ (T_1)

Next, we take Message 1 and Message 2 as,

Message 1: user$\rightarrow$ Server: A, R_1, R_2, T_1: $\{A, ID_{ia}, R_1, R2, T_1\}_B$

By applying seeing rule, we get

S1: Server ◁ A, R_1, R_2, T_1: { A, ID_{ia}, R_1, R_2, T_1}$_B$

According to S1, A3 and R1, we get

S2: Server $\models$ user~ (A, ID_{ia}, R_1, R_2, T_1)

According to A1, S2, R4, and R2 we get

S3: Server $\models$ user $\models$ (A, ID_{ia}, R_1, R_2, T_1)

Where T_1 is the timestamp used by the user.

According to A7, S3, and Jurisdiction rule

S4: Server $\models$ (A, ID_{ia}, R_1, R_2, T_1)

According to A5, S4, and session key rule

S5: Server $\models$ user $\models$ Server $\xleftrightarrow{sk = h(p \oplus n)}$ User   Achieved (Goal 2)

According to A7, S5, and R4 rule

S6: Server $\models$ Server $\xleftrightarrow{sk = h(p \oplus n)}$ User   Achieved (Goal 1)

Taking the second idealized message as:

Message 2: Server→ user: R_3, A_n, T_{s1}: { R_3, $A_n \parallel T_{s1}$}$_B$

By applying seeing rule, we get

S7: User ◁ Server → user: R_3, A_n, T_{s1}: { R_3, $A_n \parallel T_{s1}$}$_B$

According to S7, A4 and R1, we get

S8: user $\models$ Server ~ (R_3, $A_n \parallel T_{s1}$)

According to A2, S8, R4, and R3 rules we get

S9: user $\models$ Server$\models$ (R_3, $A_n \parallel T_{s1}$)

Where, T2 is the timestamp produced by the server. so

According to A6, S9, and R4 rule

S10: user $\models (R_3, A_n \parallel T_{s1})$

According to A4, S10, and session key rule

S11: user $\models$ Server $\models$ Server $\xleftarrow{sk = h(p\oplus n)}$ User   Achieved (Goal 4)

According to A8, S11, and Jurisdiction rule

S12: User $\models$ Server $\xleftarrow{sk = h(p\oplus n)}$ User   Achieved (Goal 3)

4.4 ProVerif Implementation

It is a software package for automatically investigating the confidence of cryptographic protocols. It is also capable for given reach-ability stuffs and interactive zero-knowledge verifications. It shows us the memos declaration, observational similarity, confidentiality, traceability and verifiability can be verified using this tool. The verification of a protocol using ProVerif is useful for computer security point of view. Whenever a property cannot be verified, this tool restructures and processes the drawbacks, weaknesses and robustness of the scheme. A toolkit for the authentication of secretes information over a network communication process and also for cryptographic measurement. It is a language based toolkit derived from PROLOG uses π-calculus. The proposed scheme is formally proved using this toolkit; so that the work will best gratifies the mutual authentication and session key confidentiality. . This tool supports many cryptographic fundamentals like private key / public key encryption / decryption, hashing, RSA, Diffie-Hellman algorithm, PKI, digital signature etc.

4.4.1 Proposed Protocol Verification Using ProVerif

At the start we distinct two channels, a private channel SecCh is for the use of protected communication among user and Server while open channel PubCh is for the use of unprotected communication among user and Server.

```
(*------------ Channels -------------------*)
free SCh:channel [private].     (*Secure Channel*)
free PCh:channel.


(*--------------- Constants & Variables ---------------*)
```

```
free IDia:bitstring.

free PWia:bitstring [private].

free BTia:bitstring [private].

free S:bitstring [private].


(*-------------- Constructor ----------------*)

fun H(bitstring):bitstring.

fun h(bitstring):bitstring.

fun XOR(bitstring,bitstring):bitstring.

fun CONCAT(bitstring,bitstring):bitstring.

fun E(bitstring,bitstring):bitstring.


(*------------- Destructors & Equations ----------------*)

equation forall a:bitstring,b:bitstring; XOR(XOR(a,b),b)=a.

reduc forall m:bitstring,key:bitstring; D(E(m,key),key)=m.


(*--------------------- Events ---------------------------*)

event beginUserUi(bitstring).

event endUserUi(bitstring).

event beginServerSIP(bitstring).

event endServerSIP(bitstring).



(*--------------------- Queries ---------------------------*)

free SK:bitstring [private].

query attacker(SK).
```

query id:bitstring; inj-event(endUserUi(id)) ==> inj-event(beginUserUi(id)) .

query id:bitstring; inj-event(endServerSIP(id)) ==> inj-event(beginServerSIP(id)) .

(*-------------------- User Ui --------------------*)

let UserUi=

(*-------------------- Registration -----------------*)

new q:bitstring;

let HB = H(BTia) in

let M = XOR(HB,q) in

let N = XOR(PWia,(IDia,M)) in

let O =XOR(h(XOR(PWia,(IDia,M))),q) in

out(SCh,(HB, N , IDia));

in(SCh,(xA:bitstring, xF:bitstring));

let P =h(N) in

(*--------------- Login and Authentication -------------------*)

event beginUserUi(IDia);

new IDia':bitstring;

new PWia':bitstring;

new BTia':bitstring;

let HB' = H(BTia') in

let q' = XOR(O,h(XOR(PWia',(IDia',HB')))) in

let N' = XOR(PWia',(IDia',HB',q')) in

let P' =h(N') in

if (P = P') then

```
let (B:bitstring) = D(xF,N') in

new T1:bitstring;

let R1 = h(CONCAT(B,(IDia',T1))) in

let R2 = E(CONCAT(P',(IDia',R1,T1)),B) in

out(PCh,(xA, R1, R2, T1));

in(PCh,(xR3:bitstring, xAn:bitstring, xTs1:bitstring));

let (xn:bitstring,xSK:bitstring,xTs1:bitstring) = D(xR3,B) in

let SK = h(XOR(P',xn)) in

if(SK = xSK) then

event endUserUi(IDia)

else

0.



(*-------------------- Server SIP --------------------*)

let ServerSIP=

(*---- Registration ----*)

in(SCh,(xHB:bitstring, xN:bitstring , xIDia:bitstring));

new ts0:bitstring;

let A = E(CONCAT(IDia,ts0),S) in

let B = E(XOR(IDia,S),S) in

let F =E(B,xN) in

out(SCh,(A, F));

(*---- Login and Authentication ----*)

event beginServerSIP(S);

in(PCh,(xA:bitstring, xR1:bitstring, xR2:bitstring, xT1:bitstring));
```

```
let (xIDia:bitstring,xtsO:bitstring) = D(A,S) in
let B' = E(XOR(xIDia,S),S) in


let R1' = h(CONCAT(B',(xIDia,xT1))) in


if (xR1 = R1') then
let (xP:bitstring,xIDia:bitstring,xR1:bitstring,xT1:bitstring)= D(xR2,B') in
new n:bitstring;
let SK = h(XOR(xP,n)) in
new Ts1:bitstring;
let R3 = E(CONCAT(n,(SK,Ts1)),B') in
let An = E(CONCAT(xIDia,Ts1),S) in
out(PCh,(R3, An, Ts1));
event endServerSIP(S)
else
0.


process
((!UserUi) | (!ServerSIP) )
```

The above mentioned program has been executed on ProVerif 1.93. The following result has been displayed.

-- Query inj-event(endServerSIP(id)) ==> inj-event(beginServerSIP(id))
Completing...
Starting query inj-event(endServerSIP(id)) ==> inj-event(beginServerSIP(id))
RESULT inj-event(endServerSIP(id)) ==> inj-event(beginServerSIP(id)) is true.

-- Query inj-event(endUserUi(id_624)) ==> inj-event(beginUserUi(id_624))
Completing...
Starting query inj-event(endUserUi(id_624)) ==> inj-event(beginUserUi(id_624))
RESULT inj-event(endUserUi(id_624)) ==> inj-event(beginUserUi(id_624)) is true.
-- Query not attacker(SK[])
Completing...
Starting query not attacker(SK[])
RESULT not attacker(SK[]) is true.

The above result shows that both the server and user progressions beginning and ending successfully, also confirms that the session key not exposed to an attacker. Therefore, the confidentiality is preserved.

4.5 Informal Security Analysis

In this part of the chapter, we briefly discuss the security and accuracy of our scheme mentioned in chapter 3 along with similar conventions as mentioned the last section of Chapter 2 (problem statement). Our exploration demonstrates that the recommended scheme is strong contrary to all well-known attacks. Consider an adversary can intercept a system in all communication routes, and can change, copy portions of communications information, replay messages, or release incorrect material etc. This assumption is shared for everyone and also extra sensible for now-a-days. Informal security analysis of our scheme is discussed here in this part. The following are some possible attacks discussion for our proposed scheme.

4.5.1 Denning-Sacco Attack

Let suppose an attacker gets the previous session key sk, he or she cannot get user PW_{ia} form it because the sk is created by two high entropy arbitrary numbers selected by the U_{ia} and the remote server S_{ia} respectively. Also the attacker couldn't guess the PW_{ia} or the remote server S_{ia} symmetric key $E_K(.)$. Therefore in simple words we can say that if an attacker negotiates a previous message regarding session definition, he or she cannot extract password from it. Furthermore, in every round of computation, a fresh sk is created subject to the U_{ia}'s chosen random number q, the attacker therefore, cannot calculate the session key sk=$h(p \oplus n)$. So the proposed protocol can resists Denning-Sacco Attack.

4.5.2 Stolen-Verifier Attack

The proposed scheme has no password matching database; therefore, if an attacker can obtain a useful message during the running session, he or she cannot verify PW_{ia} from it. Because the SIP server has no physical database for password, so the attacker even catches information couldn't predict password from it. Therefore, our scheme resists stolen-verifier attack.

4.5.3 Insider Attack

As we discussed above that the remote server has no database for password, even if an attacker can get the ID_{ia} he or she cannot steal password. Thus, the proposed scheme can resist an insider is attack.

4.5.4 Password Disclosure Attack

At the registration phase of the proposed scheme the U_{ia} relays $PW_{ia} \oplus ID_{ia} \oplus M$ values. The U_{ia} does not send the PW_{ia} to the remote server S_{ia}, because the password mixed with biometrics BT_{ia}, ID_{ia} and an arbitrary integer values. The attacker couldn't avail an opportunity to get the PW_{ia} at any stage of the computations. Therefore, the proposed protocol can resist the password disclosure attack.

4.5.5 Certified-Key Guarantee

The sk=$h(p \oplus n)$ is created subject to the arbitrary number selected by the user say p and another arbitrary number by the remote server say n randomly and independently in every session. So sk must be different for different sessions, therefore, the proposed scheme offers known key security or Certified-Key Guarantee.

4.5.6 Man-in-the-Middle Attack

The U_{ia} and S_{ia} shared sk after R_3 verification only, if the attacker tries to make its own connection with the S_{ia} he or she cannot share the sk, because the adversary have to compute and verify R_3. Furthermore, the attacker couldn't aware about PW_{ia}, ID_{ia} and the secrete N or the server private key S. Secondly, the attacker also couldn't predict the server sk and R_3, because it is difficult to find the big arbitrary integer n and the values (B, N) for extracting R_3. Thus the attacker cannot make its own independent connection with S_{ia} or U_{ia}. This means that the proposed protocol resist "man-in-the-middle attack".

4.5.7 Mutual Authentication

The server S_{ia} in addition to user U_{ia} might verify each other by authenticates sk and sk$'$ correspondingly. Therefore, the proposed scheme can reward mutual authentication.

4.5.8 Online Password Guessing Attack

The integrated tool smart card login and authentication process established for partial effort with wrong PW_{ia} and ID_{ia}. After these wrong efforts, it blocks and demands for S_{ia} interference to unlock and re-activate. The U_{ia} password is also safe through encryption $E_K(.)$ algorithm along with ID_{ia}, BT_{ia} and arbitrary number q. Therefore, without the knowledge of private key encryption the attacker cannot guess the password. If the attacker attempts to extract PW_{ia} form R_3 he or she needs to with-draw the arbitrary number n, ID_{ia} and PW_{ia} which is impossible. Therefore, the proposed protocol can resist "online password guessing attack".

4.5.9 Offline Password Guessing Attack

The arguments {A, F, O, P} has been stored in smart card during registration phase, it might not only revealed to guess by anyone but whenever stolen no one can extract these parameters, because the BioHashing technique is applied for protecting biometrics and then computed with the random arbitrary number $M=HB\oplus q$. Also with the application of XOR bitwise operation with PW_{ia} and ID_{ia}; $N= PW_{ia}\oplus ID_{ia}\oplus M$. Therefore, predicting PW_{ia} is requires to extracting three unknown parameters which is impossible. So the proposed scheme can resist offline password guessing attack.

4.5.10 Biometrics Security

In case someone negotiates the biometrics, BioHashing Technique is adopted. It is simple and pseudo-random sketching technique that is irreversible and can be generated using private key. As the BT_{ia} is first $HB=H(BT_{ia})$ and then computed with high entropy arbitrary number q, and q is protected by PW_{ia} and ID_{ia}. Furthermore, $O=h(PW_{ia}\oplus ID_{ia}\oplus M)\oplus q$ might substituted with $O= \varepsilon_\beta(q)$ where $\varepsilon(.)$ is encryption key for the enhancement of the security of an arbitrary number q. So even the attacker, if for example, gets PW_{ia} along with ID_{ia} and smart card, he or she cannot repossess BT_{ia} template. Therefore, we can say that the user biometric is extremely protected in the proposed scheme. No one can extract and negotiate it.

4.5.11 Resist Replay Attack

If an adversary intercept REQUEST $\{A, R_1, R_2, T_1\}$ message and replays some other time, it can be discouraged by the server due to timestamp or freshness embedded in it denoted by T_1. In other words, if an attacker tries to replay on REQUEST $\{A, R_1, R_2, T_1\}$, he or she needs to properly extract the random high entropy numbers p and q. And the attacker can also need to intercept information from R_2 i.e. ID_{ia}, PW_{ia} and BT_{ia} which are protected by a safe symmetric encryption function $\varepsilon(.)$.

Suppose an attacker interrupted CHALLENGE $\{R_3, A_n, T_{s1}\}$ message and replayed it later to the user, an achievable methodology has been employed in the proposed scheme, of dynamic identity technique i.e. $A_n = E_S(ID_{ia}||T_{s1})$. In this technique the U_{ia} real ID_{ia} is hidden in the session pseudonym ID_{ia}. The user after receiving the above message sudden calculates the timestamp or freshness of the message and discard the replay. Thus, the proposed scheme can counterattack for "replay attack".

4.5.12 Strong User Anonymity

The proposed authentication protocol accommodating a method of ''dynamic-ID'' in which freshness or timestamp is embedded for which a user's actual identity is concealed or changing for every time. No two sessions are initiated by a user for a single identity nor it is traceable during computations because a reasonable methodology is employed the ''dynamic ID technique $A_n = E_S(ID_{ia}||T_{s1})$ which was first presented by Das et al. in 2004. In this approach, the user's real individuality is cloaked in session alternate assumed name (pseudonym/false-name) uniqueness. Therefore, the legal user can only know the true server, while all the others over the channel get no valuable individual evidence. So, the proposed scheme is anonymous.

4.5.13 Resist Denial-of-Service Attack

As the proposed protocol is providing mutual authentication, secrete session key and resist replaying attack. Also smart card used is a factor for the proposed scheme consists of integrated self-computation tool, confirms the legitimacy of a user, U_{ia} gives his or her PW_{ia} and ID_{ia}. The Smart card at that moment validates the accuracy of ID_{ia} and PW_{ia}. If a single one among these is wrong, the smart card terminates the process. Login and authentication demand is subject to S_{ia} if U_{ia} is first validating by smart card. Thus, the proposed scheme resists "DoS attack".

4.6 Chapter Summary

As we know that, an authentication scheme or protocol is a small piece of distributed programs that offer security features to network communication channel and most schemes consists of one-way hash functions, i.e., functions that are simple to compute but infeasible to reverse with no supplementary information.

The *formal security analysis approach* to security rules, also known as the *BAN* method was introduced in [28]. Here, one-way digital hash functions, such as encryption and decryption, are idealized in order to achieve models that are more spontaneous and controllable, with theoretically better provision for computerization. Incompletely, cryptography is preserved as a nonconcrete data type: It is implicit that cryptographic stuffs can only be operated using a classified set of processes, which are administrated by some simple numerical laws.

Secondly, in *formal security analysis approach* another method is used in this chapter called ProVerif implementation [29-30], an automated software toolkit for implementing the proposed scheme. The result shows that the protocols that are secure in a certain formal model are also secure in a certain computational model.

While the *informal security analysis approach* prove a conceptual proof that if an adversary can active in a communication line for getting the legal information, is he or she able to abolish or expose it or not. So, we use an informal proof in this chapter that the adversary cannot do it.

Chapter 5: Performance Analysis

5.1 Overview

Performance is a character for associating unlike methods to resolving computing problem. This character can be measured along several extents, like computation throughput and communication invisibility (performance), and authority attraction and value (cost). So, performance and cost are cross-cutting features that relate to all research guidelines in computer science. Moreover, to understand the performance and cost of a specific methodology is the initial phase towards improving it, but understanding both performance and cost is frequently a challenging tasks. For methodologies that have been applied on existing schemes, gaining such thoughtful knowledge that may involve quantity and analysis. For situations somewhere the hardware or software under concern does not yet be present, performance calculation is using systematic demonstration or simulation may be essential.

In this chapter we analyzes the performance of the proposed user authentication scheme in the following terms

1. Attack Resistance and Functionality
2. Storage Overhead
3. Computation Cost
4. Communication Cost

5.1.1 Attack Resistance and Functionality Analysis

The attack resistance and functionality analysis of the proposed authentication scheme are compared with other authentication schemes namely Lee et al.'s scheme [13], Lue et al.'s scheme [14], Zhang et al.'s scheme [15], Wu et al.'s scheme [19-20], and Kumari et al.'s scheme [26].

The comparison result are list in Table 1 below, where we can determine that our proposed user authentication scheme provide resistance to all well-known attacks which in terms shows robustness, privacy preserving and strongly recommended authentication scheme. The Table 18 shown below best explains the performance and comparison analysis of the new authentication scheme.

Table- 18: The Functionality Comparison

Schemes ⟶ Security Properties	[13]	[14]	[15]	[19-20]	[26]	Proposed
Resists Denning-Sacco-Attack	Yes	Yes	Yes	Yes	Yes	Yes
Resists Stolen-Verifier Attack	Yes	Yes	Yes	Yes	Yes	Yes
Resists Insider Attack	Yes	No	Yes	Yes	Yes	Yes
Resists Password Disclosure Attack	Yes	Yes	Yes	Yes	No	Yes
Resists Replay Attack	No	No	No	Yes	Yes	Yes
Strong User Anonymity	No	No	No	No	Yes	Yes`
Rests Server Spoofing Attack	Yes	Yes	Yes	Yes	No	Yes
Provides Mutual Authentication	No	Yes	Yes	Yes	Yes	Yes
Provides Certified-Key Guarantee	Yes	Yes	Yes	Yes	Yes	Yes
Resists Impersonation Attack	Yes	No	Yes	Yes	No	Yes

5.1.2 Storage Overhead Analysis

The memory of smart card is storing {A, F, O, P} parameters and the symmetric key pairs "p, q, S, m, n". We assume that the Symmetric Cryptographic Functions used in the proposed scheme can occupy 160 bits key length, and the length of ID_{ia} value is also 160 bits. Therefore, the storage overhead of each participant is listed in Table 2 given below:

Table- 19: Storage Overhead

Parameters	Storage Overhead (in bits)
The Parameters of Smart Card	(160+160+160+160)
{A, F, O, P}	640
Private keys, high entropy random numbers	(64+64+160+64+64)
{p, q, S, m, n}	416
User Identity ID_{ia}	160
User Password PW_{ia}	160
User Biometrics BT_{ia}	320
Total	1696

5.1.3 Computation Cost Analysis

Computation cost or computational complexity is a computer science idea that concentrates on the quantity of computing resources necessary for specific types of responsibilities. In computational complexity concept, investigators measure the types of resources that will be required for a specified type or class of task in order to categorize different categories of jobs into different levels of complexity.

However, in certain means computational costs basically its own branch of mathematical theory like to the analysis of algorithms. Some consider of this method as a measurement of how much work it would take to solve a certain problem or to accomplish a particular job. Different kinds of specialists use computational complexity research to find which parts of a job may be most hard for a computing system, or to cost out how to maximum knowledgeably complete some project.

While some designers might think through computational complexity to be inappropriate to their work, others have pointed out that well altering jobs or algorithms from a greater complexity class to a minor complexity class that can make them work much better. Systems analyst and designers who use computational complexity scheme on stuffs like nested loops, logic trees or other kinds of pulses can construct well-organized schemes with a recovered understanding of how to construct less resource-hungry processes.

To inspect and evaluate the proposed scheme by comparing computational overhead in the eyes of complexity with six recent schemes e.g. Lee et al.'s scheme [13], Lue et al.'s scheme [14], Zhang et al.'s scheme [15], Wu et al.'s scheme [19-20] and Kumari et al.'s scheme [26], our scheme is strong and efficient in terms of computational cost. Table 3 illustrates the comparison in terms computation cost.

Here t_h represents time efficiency of hash-function and $t_\oplus$ represents the time efficiency of exclusive-OR operation, then the mentioned table at the end clearly shows the differences among these schemes.

Table- 20: Computational Coast Analysis of Different Schemes

Different Schemes		[13]	[14]	[15]	[19]	[20]	[26]	Our
Phases	Participant							
Registration	User	$1t_\oplus+1t_h$	$1t_\oplus+1t_h$	$5t_\oplus+1t_h$	$3t_\oplus+1t_h$	$1t_\oplus+1t_h$	$2t_\oplus+1t_h$	$6t_\oplus+3t_h$
	Server	$1t_\oplus+5t_h$	$7t_\oplus+5t_h$	$2t_\oplus+0$	$3t_\oplus+3t_h$	$2t_\oplus+3t_h$	$3t_\oplus+3t_h$	$1t_\oplus+0$
Login and Authentication	User	$4t_\oplus+9t_h$	$6t_\oplus+13t_h$	$13t_\oplus+2t_h$	$9t_\oplus+7t_h$	$3t_\oplus+7t_h$	$10t_\oplus+6t_h$	$8t_\oplus+5t_h$
	Server	$4t_\oplus+9t_h$	$7t_\oplus+19t_h$	$9t_\oplus+3t_h$	$4t_\oplus+8t_h$	$2t_\oplus+5t_h$	$3t_\oplus+5t_h$	$2t_\oplus+2t_h$
Password Change	User	$6t_\oplus+7t_h$	$4t_\oplus+3t_h$	$7t_\oplus+1t_h$	$4t_\oplus+5t_h$	$4t_\oplus+5t_h$	$7t_\oplus+4t_h$	$8t_\oplus+3t_h$
	Server	$1t_\oplus+3t_h$	$2t_\oplus+2t_h$	0	$3t_\oplus+1t_h$	$3t_\oplus+1t_h$	$0+2t_h$	0
Total (Only Login and Authentication phases are considered)		$8t_\oplus+18t_h$	$13t_\oplus+32t_h$	$22t_\oplus+5t_h$	$13t_\oplus+15t_h$	$5t_\oplus+12t_h$	$13t_\oplus+11t_h$	$10t_\oplus+7t_h$

Furthermore, the performance analysis scheme [15] some parameters can be pre-computed to reduce the computational cost of one-way hash function time t_h, which considered to be good but the XOR bitwise operation time is much higher than our scheme. Also if any function completed taking less time than a higher clock frequency is used for resource implementation. In this way the computational complexity of the proposed scheme is much better then among all. Therefore, our scheme shows good performance.

5.1.4 Communication Cost Analysis

The maximum and essential feature in data communication systems is communication cost analysis a part of power consumption via constraints peers, its comparison, its wait time, etc. In statistic, communication cost in networks is greater than computation cost in relations of power consumption. The specified proclamations best explain analysis of the communication cost of the proposed scheme. When a legitimate user login into SIP-Server using network it is easy to imagine that the proposed scheme is somewhere same as the schemes in [13-15], [20] and [26] while somewhere stronger user login and authentication. Similarly in our protocol requires a single round-trip for completion, whereas the other schemes require two or three round-trip for message exchanges, respectively. Therefore, the proposed scheme is simple and effective in improving the security over communication networks.

Let suppose the length of each parameter in the proposed scheme be 160 bits, the one-way hash function values is 256 bits and the operation performing by *XOR* on a *value* against itself always yields zero. The communication cost in the login and authentication scheme of the proposed scheme can be calculated is in Table 4 below:

	Message	Communication Overhead/cost
Step 1:	REQUEST {A, R_1, R_2, T_1}	160+416+160+64 = 800
Step 2:	CHALLENGE {R_3, A_n, T_{s1}}	416+160+64 = 640
	Total:	**1440**

From this the communication cost of our scheme is relatively small compared [13-15, 19-20, 26] schemes.

5.2 Chapter Summary

In this chapter we mainly focused on the performance of the proposed authentication scheme i.e. computation cost, storage overhead, functionality analysis and communication cost. All results for the features show that our scheme is lightweight in all respect.

Chapter 6: Conclusion and Future Work

Internet systems such as VoIP and Web applications will continue growing in size and complexity to support a larger number of users and richer functionality. Mobile platforms such as smart phones are rapidly becoming the main medium to access and consume Internet content. This trend means that users will be generating more requests to Internet applications due to the always-connected nature of smart phones. Similarly, the adoption of ubiquitous computing technologies (e.g., smart devices, wearable computing, in-car computing, etc.) will also increase the number and type of requests that need to be processed by Internet applications. The entire request load generated by applications needs to be properly handled by taking into account not only the requirements of Internet applications but also the constraints of clients' platforms. As the threat level against Internet application increases and powerful adversaries try to compromise these systems, the security of Internet applications cannot longer be considered a secondary goal. Therefore, more robust security mechanisms that satisfy the performance and scalability of large-scale Internet applications are needed. In this dissertation we have demonstrated that there is no inherent conflict between implementing robust authentication protocols and the unprecedented performance and scalability requirements of large-scale Internet applications. We have shown that by taking into account factors such as network latency, server state requirements, network bandwidth, response times and deployment costs, we can design and implement practical authentication protocols that offer stronger security guarantees than currently deployed mechanisms, while satisfying the performance and scalability constraints of large-scale VoIP and Web applications.

In this research work we are also using symmetric encryption algorithms which are the basis of diverse restrictions. The key objective was to examine the functioning of the many common private key algorithms in relationships of authentication, tractability, consistency, strength, scalability, security and to focus on the main weakness of the cited algorithms, creating each algorithm's robustness and weaknesses transparently for application. Through this study it was detected that the recommended three-factor authentication scheme was the finest amongst all others in terms of security, flexibility, robustness, reliability, scalability, memory usage and encryption presentation or encryption performance. While the remaining algorithms were also proficient but maximum of them have a compromise among storage overhead, communication and computation cost and encryption performance with few algorithms been conceded.

A biometric cryptosystem was also offered which does not considerably decline the performance of algorithm used for feature withdrawal. Motionless, the biometric cryptosystem pelts and repossesses cryptographic key in and out of biometric shape which is appropriately extensive to use in a typical cryptographic system. Moreover, maximum security can also be attained through simple means.

Furthermore, due to low computation and communication cost and more portability of smart card, commonly implemented to record individual sensitive personal information for far-flung authentication. Maximum remote user authentication protocols are now-a-days using smart cards that were familiarized previously which cannot assurance the superiority of performance for smart cards. In this dissertation, we categorized the security measures of remote user authentication protocol using smart card to fulfill all of the principles for common protocol designing. The proposed authentication protocol not only organizes the low computation and communication cost requirement, but it can survive replay and DoS attacks as well. Still, the proposed remote user authentication protocol neither needs any password table for confirmation nor clock synchronization among user and server whereas verifying mutual authentication and individuality of legal smart cards.

In future work, we will consider the other authentication schemes to find out its type and its robustness to decide the proper mechanism by using a general phenomenon / framework to overcome the chances of attacks. How to find out an attack on a scheme and what knowledge or experienced is required?

In the future, we will also plan to extend this three-factor security authentication scheme using ECC – Method, PKI – Method and DLP – Method.

Bibliography

[1] L.Lamport, "Password authentication with insecure communication," *Communications of the ACM*, Vol. 24, no, 11, pp.770-772, **1981**.

[2] Chang, C-C., and S-J. Hwang."Using smart cards to authenticate remote passwords." *Computers & Mathematics with Applications* 26, no. 7, pp.19-27, **1993**.

[3] W.C.Ku, "A hash-based strong-password authentication scheme without using smart cards," *ACM Operating System Review*, vol. 38, no. 1, pp. 29-34, **2004**.

[4] Kim, Minho, and Cetin Kaya Koç. "A Simple Attack on a Recently Introduced Hash-based Strong-password Authentication Scheme." *IJ Network Security* 1, no. 2, pp.77-80, **2005**.

[5] He, Daojing, Maode Ma, Yan Zhang, Chun Chen, and Jiajun Bu. "A strong user authentication scheme with smart cards for wireless communications."*Computer Communications* 34, no. 3, pp. 367-374, **2011**.

[6] Wu, Chia-Chun, Wei-Bin Lee, and Woei-JiunnTsaur. "A secure authentication scheme with anonymity for wireless communications." *IEEE Communications Letters* 12, no. 10, pp.722-723, **2008**.

[7] Park, Minsu, Hyunsung Kim, and Sung-Woon Lee. "Privacy Preserving Biometric-Based User Authentication Protocol Using Smart Cards."In*Computational Science and Engineering (CSE), 2014 IEEE 17th International Conference on*, pp. 1541-1544. IEEE, **2014**.

[8] Hwang, Min-Shiang, Song-Kong Chong, and Te-Yu Chen. "DoS-resistant ID-based password authentication scheme using smart cards." *Journal of Systems and Software* 83, no. 1, pp.63-172, **2010**.

[9] An, Younghwa. "Security analysis and enhancements of an effective biometric-based remote user authentication scheme using smart cards."*BioMed Research International"*, **2012**.

[10] Das, ManikLal, AshutoshSaxena, and Ved P. Gulati. "A dynamic ID-based remote user authentication scheme." *Consumer Electronics, IEEE Transactions on* 50, no. 2, pp.629-631, **2004**.

[11] Xu, Jing, Wen-Tao Zhu, and Deng-GuoFeng. "An improved smart card based password authentication scheme with provable security." *Computer Standards & Interfaces* 31, no. 4, pp.723-728, **2009**.

Bibliography

[12] Song, Ronggong. "Advanced smart card based password authentication protocol." *Computer Standards & Interfaces* 32, no. 5, pp.321-325, **2010**.

[13] Lee, Cheng-Chi, Tsung-Hung Lin, and Rui-Xiang Chang. "A secure dynamic ID based remote user authentication scheme for multi-server environment using smart cards." *Expert Systems with Applications* 38, no. 11m pp.13863-13870, **2011**.

[14] Leu, Jenq-Shiou, and Wen-Bin Hsieh. "Efficient and secure dynamic ID-based remote user authentication scheme for distributed systems using smart cards." *Information Security, IET* 8, no. 2, pp.104-113, **2014**.

[15] Zhang, Liping, Shanyu Tang, and Shaohui Zhu. "A lightweight privacy preserving authenticated key agreement protocol for SIP-based VoIP." *Peer-to-Peer Networking and Applications* 9, no. 1, pp.108-126, **2016**.

[16] Burrows M, Abadi M, Needham R "A logic of authentication" ACM Trans ComputSyst Vol. 08, pp. 8:18–36, **1990**.

[17] Diffie, Whitfield, and Martin E. Hellman. "New directions in cryptography."*Information Theory, IEEE Transactions on* 22, no. 6, pp.644-654, **1976**.

[18] http://prosecco.gforge.inria.fr/personal/bblanche/proverif/.

[19] Wu F, Xu L, Kumari S, Li X (2015) A novel and provably secure biometrics-based three-factor remote authentication scheme for mobile client–server networks. ComputElectr Eng. doi:10.1016/ j.compeleceng, **2015**.

[20] Wu, Fan, Lili Xu, Saru Kumari, Xiong Li, and AbdulhameedAlelaiwi. "A new authenticated key agreement scheme based on smart cards providing user anonymity with formal proof." *Security and Communication Networks* 8, no. 18, pp.3847-3863, **2015**.

[21] Tsai JL, and Lo NW. "A chaotic map-based anonymous multi-server authenticated key agreement protocol using smart card. International Journal of Communication Systems, **2014**.

[22] Zhang, Liping, Shaohui Zhu, and Shanyu Tang. "Privacy protection for telecare medicine information systems using a chaotic map-based three-factor authenticated key agreement scheme." **2016**.

[23] Hou, Young-Chang, Shih-Chieh Wei, and Chia-Yin Lin. "Random-grid-based visual cryptography schemes." *Circuits and Systems for Video Technology, IEEE Transactions on* 24, no. 5, pp.733-744, **2014**.

[24] Shen, Shu-Yuan, and Li-Hong Huang. "A data hiding scheme using pixel value differencing and improving exploiting modification directions."*Computers& Security* 48, pp.131-141, **2015**.

[25] Stallings, W. *Cryptography and network security:principles and practices, 3th edition*: Prentice Hall, **2003**.

[26] Kumari, Saru, Muhammad Khurram Khan, and Xiong Li. "An improved remote user authentication scheme with key agreement." Computers & Electrical Engineering, Vol. 40, No 6, pp 1997-2012, **2014**.

[27] M. Blum and S. Micali. How to generate cryptographically strong sequences of pseudo random bits. In *23rd Annual Symposium on Foundations of Computer Science, 3-5 November 1982, Chicago, Illinois, USA*, pages 112–117. IEEE, **1982**.

[28] Burrows M, Abadi M, Needham R "A logic of authentication" ACM Trans ComputSyst Vol. 08, pp. 8:18–36, **1990**.

[29] S. Goldwasser and S. Micali. Probabilistic encryption. *J. Comput. Syst. Sci.*, 28(2):270–299, **1984**.

[30] Bruno Blanchet, Mart´ın Abadi, and C´edric Fournet. Automated verification of selected equivalences for security protocols. Journal of Logic and Algebraic Programming, 75(1):3–51, February–March **2008**.

[31] Liqun Chen and Mark Ryan. Attack, solution and verification for shared authorisation data in TCG TPM. In Proc. Sixth Formal Aspects in Security and Trust (FAST'09), volume 5983 of Lecture Notes in Computer Science. Springer, **2009**.

[32] Chen, Huifang, Linlin Ge, and Lei Xie. "A User Authentication Scheme Based on Elliptic Curves Cryptography for Wireless Ad Hoc Networks."*Sensors* 15, no. 7, pp:17057-17075, **2015**.

[33] Abbas, Sohail, Madjid Merabti, and David Llewellyn-Jones. "Signal strength based Sybil attack detection in wireless Ad Hoc networks." In *Developments in eSystems Engineering (DESE), 2009 Second International Conference on*, pp. 190-195. IEEE, **2009**.

[34] Abbas, Sohail, Madjid Merabti, and David Llewellyn-Jones. "Deterring whitewashing attacks in reputation based schemes for mobile ad hoc networks." In *Wireless Days (WD), 2010 IFIP*, pp. 1-6. IEEE, **2010**.

[35] Abbas, Sohail, Madjid Merabti, and David Llewellyn-Jones. "A Survey of Reputation Based Schemes for MANET." In *The 11th Annual Conference on the Convergence of Telecommunications, Networking & Broadcasting (PGNet 2010), Liverpool, UK*, pp. 21-22. **2010**.

[36] Abbas, Sohail, Madjid Merabti, and David Llewellyn-Jones. "The effect of direct interactions on reputation based schemes in mobile ad hoc networks." In *Consumer Communications and Networking Conference (CCNC), 2011 IEEE*, pp. 297-302. IEEE, **2011**.

[37] Khan, Jamil Y., Mehmet R. Yuce, and Farbood Karami. "Performance evaluation of a wireless body area sensor network for remote patient monitoring." 30th IEEE Annual International Conference of the Engineering in Medicine and Biology Society, pp 1266-1269, **2008**.

[38] Mana, Mohammed, Mohammed Feham, and Boucif Amar Bensaber. "Trust Key Management Scheme for Wireless Body Area Networks." International Journal of Network Security Vol. 12 No 2, pp 75-83, **2011**.

[39] Keoh, Sye Loong, Emil Lupu, and Morris Sloman. "Securing body sensor networks: Sensor association and key management." IEEE International Conference on Pervasive Computing and Communications, pp 1-6, **2009**.

[40] Latre, Benoit, Bart Braem, Ingrid Moerman, Chris Blondia, Elisabeth Reusens, Wout Joseph, and Piet Demeester. "A low-delay protocol for multihop wireless body area networks." Fourth Annual International Conference on Mobile and Ubiquitous Systems: Networking & Services, pp. 1-8, **2007**.

[41] Hanson, Mark A., Harry C. Powell Jr, Adam T. Barth, Kyle Ringgenberg, Benton H. Calhoun, James H. Aylor, and John Lach. "Body area sensor networks: Challenges and opportunities." IEEE Computer Society pp 58-65, **2009**.

[42] Poon, Carmen CY, Yuan-Ting Zhang, and Shu-Di Bao. "A novel biometrics method to secure wireless body area sensor networks for telemedicine and m-health." IEEE Communications Magazine, Vol. 44, No 4, pp 73-81, **2006**.

[43] Saleem, Shahnaz, Sana Ullah, and Hyeong Seon Yoo. "On the Security Issues in Wireless Body Area Networks." International Journal of Digital Content Technology and its Applications Vol. 3, No 3, pp 178-184 **2009**.

[44] Ren, Hongliang, Max QH Meng, and Xijun Chen. "Physiological information acquisition through wireless biomedical sensor networks." IEEE International Conference on Information Acquisition, pp 483-488, **2005**.

[45] D. Mishra, S. Mukhopadhyay, A. Chaturvedi, S. Kumari, M. Khan, "Cryptanalysis and improvement of Yan et al.'s biometric-based authentication scheme for telecare medicine information systems", *J. Med. Syst.*, vol. 38, no. 6, pp. 1-12, **2014**.

[46] X. Yan, W. Li, P. Li, J. Wang, X. Hao, P. Gong, "A secure biometrics-based authentication scheme for telecare medicine information systems", *J. Med. Syst.*, vol. 37, no. 5, pp. 1-6, **2013**.

[47] Venkatasubramanian, Krishna K., Ayan Banerjee, and Sandeep Kumar S. Gupta. "PSKA: usable and secure key agreement scheme for body area networks." IEEE Transactions on Information Technology in Biomedicine, Vol. 14, No 1, pp 60-68, **2010**.

[48] Otto, Chris, Aleksandar Milenkovic, Corey Sanders, and Emil Jovanov. "System architecture of a wireless body area sensor network for ubiquitous health monitoring." Journal of Mobile Multimedia, Vol. 1, No 4, pp 307-326, **2006**.

[49] H. Arshad, M. Nikooghadam, "Three-factor anonymous authentication and key agreement scheme for telecare medicine information systems", *J. Med. Syst.*, vol. 38, no. 3, pp. 1-9, **2014**.

[50] Z. Tan. "A user anonymity preserving three-factor authentication scheme for telecare medicine information systems", *J. Med. Syst.*, vol. 38, no. 3, pp. 1-9, **2014**.

[51] D. Mishra, S. Mukhopadhyay, S. Kumari, M. Khan, A. Chaturvedi., "Security enhancement of a biometrics based authentication scheme for telecare medicine information systems with nonce", *J. Med. Syst.*, vol. 38, no. 5, pp. 1-11, **2014**.

[52] A. Awasthi, K. Srivastava, "A biometric authentication scheme for telecare medicine information systems with nonce", *J. Med. Syst.*, vol. 37, no. 5, pp. 1-7, **2013**.

[53] D. Mishra, "Understanding Security Failures of Two Authentication and Key Agreement Schemes for Telecare Medicine Information Systems". *J. Med. Syst*, doi: 10.1007/s10916-015-0193-7, **2015**.

[54] Venkatasubramanian, Krishna K., and Sandeep KS Gupta. "Physiological value-based efficient usable security solutions for body sensor networks." ACM Transactions on Sensor Networks Vol. 6, No 4, pp 1-31- 2010.

[55] M. Farash, M. Attari, "An efficient and provably secure three-party password-based authenticated key exchange protocol based on Chebyshev chaotic maps", *Nonlinear Dyn*, vol. 77, no. 1-2, pp. 399-411, **2014**.

[56] Keoh, Sye Loong. "Efficient group key management and authentication for body sensor networks." IEEE International Conference on Communications, pp 1-6, **2011**.

[57] Zhao, Zhenguo. "An efficient anonymous authentication scheme for wireless body area networks using elliptic curve cryptosystem." Journal of medical systems Vol. 38, No 2, pp 1-7, **2014**.

[58] Aftab Ali, Sarah Irum, Firdous Kausar, and Farrukh Aslam Khan. "A cluster-based key agreement scheme using keyed hashing for Body Area Networks." Multimedia tools and applications Vol. 66, No 2, pp 201-214, **2013**.

[59] Daojing He, Shing-Chow Chan, Yan Zhang, and Haomiao Yang. "Lightweight and Confidential Data Discovery and Dissemination for Wireless Body Area Networks." IEEE Journal of Biomedical and Health Informatics, Vol. 18 No 2, pp 440-448, **2014**.

[60] Al Ameen, Moshaddique, Jingwei Liu, and Kyungsup Kwak. "Security and privacy issues in wireless sensor networks for healthcare applications." Journal of medical systems, Vol. 36, No 1, pp 93-101, **2012**.

[61] Lee, Cheng-Chi, Tsung-Hung Lin, and Rui-Xiang Chang. "A secure dynamic ID based remote user authentication scheme for multi-server environment using smart cards." Expert Systems with Applications, Vol. 38, No 11, pp 13863-13670, **2011**.

[62] Leu, Jenq-Shiou, and Wen-Bin Hsieh. "Efficient and secure dynamic ID-based remote user authentication scheme for distributed systems using smart cards." IET Information Security, Vol. 8, No 2, pp 104-113, **2014**.

[63] F.T. Wen, L.D. Guo, "An improved anonymous authentication scheme for telecare medical information systems", *J. Med. Syst.*, vol. 38, no. 5, pp. 1-8, **2014**.

[64] Kumari, Saru, Muhammad Khurram Khan, and Xiong Li. "An improved remote user authentication scheme with key agreement." Computers & Electrical Engineering, Vol. 40, No 6, pp 1997-2012, **2014**.

[65] Chen, Chi-Tung, and Cheng-Chi Lee. "A two-factor authentication scheme with anonymity for multi-server environments." Security and Communication Networks, Vol. 8, No 8, pp 1608-1625, **2014**.

Bibliography

[66] Kumari, Saru, Muhammad Khurram Khan, Xiong Li, and Fan Wu. "Design of a user anonymous password authentication scheme without smart card." International Journal of Communication Systems, DOI. 10.1002/dac.2853, **2014**.

[67] Xie, Qi, Na Dong, Duncan S. Wong, and Bin Hu. "Cryptanalysis and security enhancement of a robust two-factor authentication and key agreement protocol." International Journal of Communication Systems, DOI. 10.1002/dac.2858, **2014**.

[68] L.P. Zhang, S.Y. Tang, S.H. J. Chen, Zhu, "Two-factor remote authentication protocol with user anonymity based on elliptic curve cryptography", *Wireless personal communications*, vol. 81, no. 1, pp. 53-75, **2015**.

[69] L.P. Zhang, S.H., Zhu, "Robust ECC-based authenticated key agreement scheme with privacy protection for Telecare Medicine Information Systems", *Journal of Medical System*, vol. 39, no. 5, pp. 1-13, **2015**.

[70] Yang, Guomin, Duncan S. Wong, Huaxiong Wang, and Xiaotie Deng. "Two-factor mutual authentication based on smart cards and passwords." *Journal of Computer and System Sciences* 74, no. 7, pp.1160-1172, **2008**.

[71] Fan, Chun-I., and Yi-Hui Lin. "Provably secure remote truly three-factor authentication scheme with privacy protection on biometrics." *Information Forensics and Security, IEEE Transactions on* 4, no. 4, pp.933-945, **2009**.

[72] R. Amin, G.P. Biswas, "A secure three-factor user authentication and key agreement protocol for tmis with user anonymity", *J. Med. Syst*, vol. 39, no. 8, **2015**.

[73] Maurer, Ueli. "Modelling a public-key infrastructure." In *Computer Security— ESORICS 96*, pp. 325-350. Springer Berlin Heidelberg, **1996**.

[74] Goode, Bur. "Voice over internet protocol (VoIP)." *Proceedings of the IEEE* 90, no. 9, pp.1495-1517, **2002**.

[75] Rosenberg, Jonathan, Henning Schulzrinne, Gonzalo Camarillo, Alan Johnston, Jon Peterson, Robert Sparks, Mark Handley, and Eve Schooler.*SIP: session initiation protocol*. Vol. 23. RFC 3261, Internet Engineering Task Force, **2002**.

[76] Basem, Basma, Atef Z. Ghalwash, and Rowayda A. Sadek. "Multilayer Secured SIP Based VoIP Architecture." *International Journal of Computer Theory and Engineering* 7, no. 6, pp. 453, **2015**.

[77] Thom, Gary A. "H. 323: the multimedia communications standard for local area networks." *Communications Magazine, IEEE* 34, no. 12, pp. 52-56, **1996**.

[78] Husemann, Dirk. "The smart card: don't leave home without it." *Concurrency, IEEE* 7, no. 2, pp.24-27, **1999**.

[79] F. Zhao, P. Gong, S. Li, M. Li, P. Li, "Cryptanalysis and improvement of a three-party key agreement protocol using enhanced Chebyshev polynomials", *Nonlinear Dyn*, vol. 74, no. 1-2, pp. 419-427, **2013**.

[80] X. Xu, P. Zhu, Q.Y. Wen, Z.P. Jin, H. Zhang, L. He, "A secure and efficient authentication and key agreement scheme based on ECC for telecare medicine information system", *J. Med. Syst.*, vol. 38, no. 1, pp. 1-7, **2014**.

[81] T.F. Lee, "Verifier-based three-party authentication schemes using extended chaotic maps for data exchange in telecare medicine information systems", *Comput. Methods Progr. Biomed.*, vol. 117, no.3, pp. 464-472, **2014**.

[82] T.F. Lee, C.M. Liu, "A secure smart-card based authentication and key agreement scheme for telecare medicine information systems", *J. Med. Syst.*, vol. 37, no. 3, pp. 1-11, **2013**.

[83] Y.C. Yu, T.W. Hou, "An efficient forward-secure certificate digital signature scheme to enhance EMR authentication process", *Med. Biol. Eng. Comput.*, vol.52, pp. 449–457, **2014**.

[84] M.K. Khan, K. Alghathbar, Cryptanalysis and security improvements of two-factor user authentication in wireless sensor networks, Sen- sors 10 (3), pp.2450–2459, **2010**.

[85] D. He, Y. Gao, S. Chan, C. Chen, J. Bu ,An enhanced two-factor user authentication scheme in wireless sensor networks, Ad Hoc Sensor Wirel. Netw. 10 (4), pp.361–371, **2010**.

[86] B. Vaidya, D. Makrakis, H.T. Mouftah, Improved two-factor user au- thentication in wireless sensor networks, in: Proceedings of the IEEE 6th International Conference on Wireless and Mobile Computing, Networking and Communications (WiMob'10), pp.600–606, **2010**.

[87] R. Fan , L.-d. Ping , J.-Q. Fu , X.-Z. Pan , A secure and efficient user authentication protocol for two-tiered wireless sensor networks, in: Proceedings of the Second Pacific-Asia Conference on Cir- cuits,Communications and System (PACCS'10), vol. 1, pp. 425–428, **2010**.

[88] V. Slavov, P. Rao, S. Paturi, T.K. Swami, M. Barnes, D. Rao, R. Palvai. "A new tool for sharing and querying of clinical documents modeled using HL7 Version 3 standard", *Comput. Methods Progr. Biomed.*, vol. 112, no. 3, pp. 529–552, **2013**.

[89] J. Yuan , C. Jiang , Z. Jiang , A biometric based user authentication for wireless sensor networks, Wuhan Univ. J. Nat. Sci. 15 (3), pp.272–276, **2010**.

[90] P. Kumar , H.-J. Lee , Cryptanalysis on two user authentication proto- cols using smart card for wireless sensor networks, in: Proceedings of the Wireless Advanced (WiAd'11), pp. 241–245, **2011**.

[91] A.K. Das , P. Sharma , S. Chatterjee , J.K. Sing , A dynamic password- based user authentication scheme for hierarchical wireless sensor networks, J. Netw. Comput. Appl. 35 (5), pp.646–1656, **2012**.

[92] K. Xue , C. Ma , P. Hong , R. Ding ,A temporal-credential-based mutual authentication and key agreement scheme for wireless sensor net- works, J. Netw. Comput. Appl. 36 (1), pp.316–323, **2013** .

[93] S. Xu , X. Wang , A new user authentication scheme for hierarchical wireless sensor networks, Int. Rev. Comput. Softw. 8 (6) (2013) 197–203 . [31] M. Turkanovi´c , M. Hölbl , An improved dynamic password-based user authentication scheme for hierarchical wireless sensor networks, Elektronika Ir Elektrotechnika 19 (6), pp.109–116, **2013** .

[94] C.-T. Li , C.-Y. Weng , C.-C. Lee , An advanced temporal credential-based security scheme with mutual authentication and key agreement for wireless sensor networks, Sensors 13 (8), pp.9589–9603, **2013** .

[95] D. He , N. Kumar , N. Chilamkurti , A secure temporal-credential-based mutual authentication and key agreement scheme with pseudo iden- tity for wireless sensor networks, Inf. Sci. 321, pp.263–277, **2015** .

[96] D. Wang , P. Wang , Understanding security failures of two-factor au- thentication schemes for real-time applications in hierarchical wire- less sensor networks, Ad Hoc Netw. 20, pp.1–15, **2014**.

[97] R. Amin , G.P. Biswas , A secure light weight scheme for user authen- tication and key agreement in multi-gateway based wireless sensor networks, Ad Hoc Netw. 36, pp.58–80, **2016** .

[98] L. Nguyen, E. Bellucci, "Electronic health records implementation: An evaluation of information system impact and contingency factors", *Int. J. Med. Inf.*, vol. 83, no. 11, pp. 779-796, **2014**.

[99] C. Esposito, M. Ciampi, G. Pietro, "An event-based notification approach for the delivery of patient medical information", *Inform. Syst.*, vol.39, pp. 22-44, **2014**.

[100] Y.-F. Chang , S.-H. Yu , D.-R. Shiao , A uniqueness-and-anonymity- preserving remote user authentication scheme for connected health care, J. Med. Syst. 37 (2), pp.9902, **2013**.

[101] L. Leng , A.T.B. Jin , M. Li , M.K. Khan , A remote cancelable palmprint authentication protocol based on multi-directional two- dimensional palmphasor-fusion, Secur. Commun. Netw. 7 (11), pp.1860–1871, **2014**.

[102] L. Leng , A.T.B. Jin , Alignment-free row-co-occurrence cancelable palmprint fuzzy vault, Pattern Recognit. 48 (17), pp.2290–2303, **2015**.

[103] A. Armando , D. Basin , Y. Boichut , Y. Chevalier , L. Compagna , J. Cuellar , P. Drielsma , P.C. HeÈím , O. Kouchnarenko , J. Mantovani , S. MÈμdersheim , D. von Oheimb , M. Rusinowitch , J. Santiago , M. Tu- ruani , L. Vigan , L. Vigneron , The AVISPA tool for the automated val- idation of internet security protocols and applications, in: Proceed- ings of the 17th International Conference on Computer Aided Verifi- cation (CAV'05), in: *LNCS* , vol. 3576, pp. 281–285, **2005**.

[104] W.B. Lee, C.D Lee, K.I. Ho, "A HIPAA-compliant key management scheme with revocation of authorization", *Comput. Methods Progr. Biomed.*, vol. 113, no. 3, pp. 809–814, **2014**.

CURRICULUM VITAE

Saeed Ullah Jan

Lecturer in Computer Science, Higher Education Department
Govt: of Khyber Pakhtunkhwa at Govt Degree College Wari Upper Dir 18200 – Pakistan
+923449222133 saeedullah@uom.edu.pk, saeedjan03@gmail.com

Educational Qualification

Degree	Session / Registration No.	CGPA / Grade	Institution
MPhil Computer Science	2013-2015/ 20020010003	3.23/4 A	University of Malakand Chakdara – Malakand
	Courses Studied: Advance Operating System ‖ Advance Analysis of Algorithm Advance Computer Architecture ‖ Advance Theory of Computation Software Re-Engineering ‖ Software Re-Factoring Software Engineering Aspects of Green Computing Evolutionary Computation ‖ Cryptography & Network Security Research Methods in Computer Science ‖ Advance Topics in Networking		
Dissertation Title	An Improved Lightweight Privacy Preserving Authentication Scheme for SIP-Based-VoIP using Smart Card		

2- University of Malakand, Chakdara, Khyber Pakhtunkhwa

- Degree: BS(CS) 04-06-2007   **04 Year Degree Program (16 Years of Education)**
- Major in Computer Science
- Percentage 79.23/100 ‖ Marks 2773/3500
- Session 2002 – 2006
- Registration No. 20020010003

3- BISE Peshawar, Khyber Pakhtunkhwa   01 Year Certificate Program

- Certificate in Mathematics (Additional) 03-09-2002
- Major in Mathematics
- Percentage 79.50/100 ‖ Marks 159/200

4- BISE Peshawar, Khyber Pakhtunkhwa

- F.Sc (Pre-Medical) 30-03-2001   **02 Year Certificate Program (12 Years of Education)**
- Major in Physics, Biology, Chemistry, Urdu, English
- Percentage 71.54/100 ‖ Marks 787/1100

5- BISE Peshawar, Khyber Pakhtunkhwa

- SSC (Science) 25-05-1998   **02 Year Certificate Program (10 Years of Education)**
- Major in Physics, Mathematics, Biology, Chemistry, Urdu, English
- Percentage 68.58/100 ‖ Marks 583/850

Experience 01-08-2007 – To – Present

Position: Lecturer in Computer Science || Employer: Higher Education Department Govt of Khyber Pakhtunkhwa (www.hed.gkp.pk)

Station 1: Govt Degree College Kotha Sawabi District Sawabi (2007-2008)
Station 2: Govt Degree College Chitral District Chitral (2008-2012)
Station 3: Govt Degree College Wari District Upper Dir (2012- to date)

RESPONSIBILITIES

Teaching "Data Communication and Networking, Introduction to Operating System, Introduction to Database, Digital Logic & Computer Design, Data Structure, Introduction to Discrete Mathematics, C – Programming Language, C++ Programming language, Object Oriented Programming in C++, MS – Word, Excel, Access etc. to B.Sc and HSSC – Level students; supervising different projects and thesis of BS – level students.

Sr.No.	PROFESSIONAL ACTIVITIES	WORK NATURE / RESPONSIBILITIES
01	**Controller of Examinations** August, 2012 – to – Date	1. All matters concerned with the conduct of Pre-Board and Pre-University examinations. 2. Issuing date sheet, appointment of supervisory staff, allocating examination center(s) and issuance of admit cards to students. 3. Preparation and display of final result notification (s) and sending the grade reports to students' parents. 4. Arrangement for the timely issuance/provision of the examination material, instructing the supervisory staff and holding their meetings as and when required. 5. Postponement or cancellation of examination, in part or in whole, in the event of malpractices or if the circumstances so warrant after approval of the undersigned. 6. Appointment of unfair means (UFM) committee with prior approval of Principal GDC Wari in relation to examination matters for carrying out investigation and convenes meeting and issue notices thereof. 7. Maintaining over all examinations record of the students. 8. Ensuring and maintaining strict secrecy of all information regarding the examinations.
02	**Focal Person:** Emergency Services Mar, 2012 – to – Date	Fully Operational of Android Cell Phone for SOS – Emergency Services (one click SMS Alert System Handling Activities) CCTV – Cameras Backup Maintenances & Operating Activities
03	**Focal Person:** Higher Education Management Information System (HEMIS) – Cell Nov, 2014 – to – Date	Student Information, budget Record, Professors / Lecturers Complete record, Commodities information, building and facilities information. Managing Web and Database Administrator's activities URL: http://www.mis.hed.gkp.pk

04	**Focal Person:** Biometric Based Attendance Monitoring System (BBAMS) – Wing HED Sep, 2016 – to – Date	According to Section 6 of the Standard Operating Procedures (SOP's) "The Controlling Officer shall take appropriate steps for the appointment of focal person from the existing faculty or any of the college staff who is friendly with the software or who has task of maintaining data related matters need an exclusive professional. The Competent Authority gives me the responsibility of operating BBAMS for GDC Wari (Dir Upper). URL: http://103.240.220.73:73/ams/signin.aspx
05	**Web Administrator:** Official Website of the College Mar, 2017 – to – Date	Implemented Online Admission System, information to be provided to all students and general public, admission rules, discipline rules, College rules & regulations Uploading of E – Prospectus, admission policy and other necessary information on the website that facilitate the students and general public.
06	**Dy: Chief Proctor** Session 2013 – 2014	I worked two consecutive sessions for marinating peace inside the college premises, issuance of ID – Cads to the regular students. Then left for the incoming junior's Lecturers
07	**Warden:** Boys Hostel Session 2012, 2013, 2014 & 2015	Overall management of hostel related issues in the evening time for those students whose living in the hostel. Now I shifted with my family to the local town, so leave it for the junior staff members.
08	**Member:** College Council March, 2012 – to – Date	A 3-tier management system has been introduced, for effective policy-making and close co-ordination between the Colleges and Directorate, consisting of: - College Council, Joint Management Council and Provincial Management Council
09	**Nominee:** Departmental Selection Committee Feb, 2016	A committee for the initial appointment/recruitment of Employee(s) in the institutions. At most three (3) officer will be in the committee 1. Appointing Authority (Principal) 2. Nominee No. 1 (Director or Dy: Director Colleges) 3. Nominee No. 2 (Selects by the appointing authority from the existing staff) & I have been nominated.
10	**Chairman:** Admission Committee Academic Session 2013, 2014, 2015 & 2016	Chaired different admission committees at both HSSC BS/and BSc Levels in different academic sessions.
11	**Chairman:** Purchase Committee Financial Year, 2013, 2014, 2015 & 2016	Supervise purchase processes: e.g. tender, comparing different rates. Select the lowest one, issuing supply order, ensuring supply, quality and quantity.
12	**Chairman:** Physical Verification Committee Dec, 2014, 2015 & 2016	Every year at the end of the session, physical verification of items, equipment's etc. were ensured by the head from a trusted official, and I am the one which for the said task continuously in order to ensure all the items/equipment. Lab gears and Machinery including all public property for the college.

13	**Incharge:** Teaching Assistants Nov, 2014 – to – Date	1. Incharge for the newly appointed Teaching Assistants 2. Officially verifying their documents form the concerned Universities 3. Take a written bond from him on behalf of Govt of Khyber Pakhtunkhwa 4. Releasing their salaries, supervising their work and submitting monthly progress report based on their performance. Assigning different tasks to them time by time
14	**Supervisor:** National Internship Program (PM – Youth Scheme) August, 2016 – to – Date	1. Ensuring the submission of Intern Assessment Reports of all interns in the organization by 24th of every month positively. 2. Assign Tasks to the Intern, check their performance and report to the cluster Incharge URL: http://monitoring.nip.gov.pk

Awards and Acknowledgments
- The Provincial Govt of Khyber Pakhtunkhwa grants me Rs: 200000/- for the successful completion of M.Phil - Degree.
- I am the Pioneer student to complete M.Phil Computer Science from CS&IT Department
- I designed a SIP-Based-VoIP Authentication Protocol
- I got 4th Position out of 31 in BS – Computer Science Degree Program
- Average Passing percentage of my students for the last 08 years is 87.11%

Dissertation / Article Titles
- MPhil Thesis Title: An Improved Lightweight Privacy Preserving Authentication Scheme for SIP-Based-VoIP using Smart Card. (Submitted)
- BS Thesis Title: Human Resource Management System for Hunza Sugar Mills Working over Local Area Network.
- Article Title: Smart Card – A Secure and Authentic eLearning Tool for Promoting Distance Learning Education (Submitted)
- Article Title: Developing the Best Scheduling Algorithm from Existing Algorithms for Real Time Operating Systems. (Published)
- Article Title: A Survey Paper on Cloud Computing – Storage Issues and Challenges (Submitted)
- Article Title: Education in the Age of Technology (Submitted)
- Article Title: A Robust Authentication Scheme for Client-Server Computing with Proper Security Analysis (Submitted)

Languages
- English, Urdu & Pashto (Read, Write & Speak)

Hobbies
- Walking, Watching Television, Reading Books, Group Discussion with Colleagues & Spent time with family.

Additional Information

- Father's Name: ZARAWAR KHAN   Date of Birth: 11-04-1981
- CNIC No.   15701-1225009-3   Passport No.   AV8790092
- Gender: Male   Nationality: Pakistani
- Domicile: Upper Dir Khyber Pakhtunkhwa
- Skype ID: saeed.ullah.jan   Twitter: @SAEEDULLAHJAN03
- Facebook Contact: https://www.facebook.com/saeed.ullah.jan03

Objectives

- I am young and energetic having pleasant personality with strong interpersonal skills, self-motivated and responsible professional appearance.
- Task oriented, flexible and adoptable and love to work in any challenging environment, where I can broaden my horizon by complementing my theoretical knowledge by practical experience.
- Looking for a responsible position with career oriented organization, having professional environment, where I can apply my experience and education background, I have the ability to work with diversified group and individuals in different environment and culture.
- I assure that I will have the capability to adapt quickly myself for any sort of environment.
- I want to work in a position where I can better utilize my experience in an appropriate manner.
- To excel in my field through hard work, research, skill and perseverance.
- To be involved in work where I can utilize my skills and abilities that effectively contribute to the growth of my organization.

References

Referee No. 1:   ***Professor Muhammad Roze Khan (Employer – Head)***
Director (Colleges) Khyber Pakhtunkhwa, Peshawar
+92 – 91 – 9210215, 9210242, 9211025, 9211803

Referee No. 2:   ***Professor Rahmat Karim (Campus – Head)***
Principal Govt Degree College Wari Dir Upper
18200 – Khyber Pakhtunkhwa, Pakistan
+92 – 944 – 840488, Cell#: +923410990003
Email: gdcwari@gmail.com

Referee No. 3:   ***Dr.Fawad Qayum (MPhil – Supervisor)***
Chairman Department of Software Engineering
MPhil/PhD – Coordinator, University of Malakand
Phone: +92 – 946 – 764132 Cell#: +923365364000
Email: fawadqayum@uom.edu.pk

Referee No. 4:   ***Dr.Ajab Khan (Research Advisor)***
Assistant Professor Department of CS & IT
Manager Research ORIC, University of Malakand
Phone: +92 – 946 – 764131 Cell#: +923445378142
Email: ajabkhan@uom.edu.pk